WHY CRY?

LaVon Mercer
with Charles Ellis Jr.

DEDICATION

To "my Village", these individuals that watered me, loved, who challenged me to live life with a purpose: Curtis & Ellroe Mercer, Louise Mercer, Curly & Jearlean Byrd, Sarah Thomas, Coach Len West, Roscoe Holland, TM Mercer, Inman Hayes, Harold Mercer, Frank & Mary Lee Hagan, Alma Toomer, Margie Horton, Dorothy "Dot" Campbell, Hilda Holloway and William George

LaVon Mercer

To my grandparents that time did not afford me an opportunity to know: Wincey Beatrice Benjamin, Herbert Mincey and Rias Ellis and the big three that I did know and who had a dramatic impact on my life: Hazel LaJuan Mincey Joiner, Hazel Dixon Benjamin and Emma Ellis Randall

Charles Ellis, Jr.

TABLE OF CONTENTS

ACKNOWLEDGMENTS

Special thanks to the following individuals for their contributions to this book: Rhea Michaela Thomas Ellis, Larry Hobbs, Darryl Robinson, Ralph Daniels, Bobby Harris and Gary Sobel

IN THE BEGINNING

"It ain't where you start in life, its where you end up,
and what you did along the way."

Colin Powell

PUSH ME WHERE MY TRUST IS WITHOUT BORDERS

I grew up in a small farming town in southeast Georgia (GA). The town of Metter is the county seat of Candler County, GA which is located about 60 miles west of Savannah and 100 miles south of Macon; the state's second largest city. In 1958 the year that I was born, Candler County consisted of about 6,700 residents and the "town" of Metter had a population of just over 2,300. Today, the county has about 11,000 residents and the population of Metter is approximately 4,100. Metter is your typical small south GA town.

When people from other states think about GA, Atlanta usually comes to mind or maybe Savannah because of its history. But GA residents typically say there is Atlanta and then there's GA. GA and particularly the southern part consists of many small rural towns generally populated with five to ten thousand people. These towns are interconnected by state and county roads and if there is any industry there, it's likely to center around farming. Farming was the predominate way of earning income in the South when I was a kid and not much has changed about that today.

Downtown Metter is basically organized around four blocks and four traffic lights all of which are within one mile. The four traffic lights are located on state road 46 which runs east and west across the state. In the 1960's and 70's when I was a kid the core stores in downtown Metter were Western Auto, Trapnell Tomlinson Ace Hardware, Bird's Pharmacy, Joe Coursey's Grocery Store, a five and dime store and the Allied Department Store. Also, interspersed around those stores were a few local restaurants and other businesses.

Other stores included a Tastee Freeze, Vernon's Minute Mart and several gas stations. Momma Sarah, who I will introduce in greater detail later in the book, owned a sewing shop in downtown Metter where she made money as an excellent seamstress. In the center of those four blocks was a beautiful fountain which accentuated the downtown landscape.

My home was about 10 to 12 miles from downtown Metter in the "Charlton Grove" community. Charlton Grove still exists today. People who live in small towns either live "in town" or "in the country." The "country" is the less populated areas outside of town that consist of paved county roads and dirt roads. I lived in the "country" and approximately two miles from the Charlton Grove Baptist Church. The "country" is where the money is made in small rural towns and communities. Everything in my world of Charlton Grove centered around the church.

If you haven't grown up in the South or especially in the "country," you probably have no idea where most of the food that you consume comes from. The "country" or the rural areas generally consist of farmland. A ride in the "country" will offer you the most scenic views of rows and rows of soybeans, peanuts, corn and other crops. In my childhood years, the most commonly planted and noticeable crop in the "country" was tobacco. In those times, smoking was very common among men and women and not taboo like it is today. So, most farms in my area and across the South made a lot of money from tobacco. The other signature crop of the South was cotton. Cotton is one of those crops that Blacks have mixed feelings about because it is a reminder of the toils of our ancestors in slavery and even after slavery as poorly paid sharecroppers. But like many things in the South, that's just how it was. Money was needed to survive so we worked in those fields harvesting cotton and tobacco to earn a living.

The school systems were segregated when I entered kindergarten, so I began in an all Black school. That would be shocking for kids today but that was nothing out of the ordinary back then; that's just how it was. We were just glad to go to school and had no real concern about there being another school with all White kids with better books and facilities. Desegregation began in the 1970's so I graduated from the integrated Metter High School instead of the Lillian Street School where Blacks before me graduated from high school. The Lillian Street School in the Black part of town was the center of the Black community in Metter. I say Black part of town because just as in most southern cities and towns, residents were separated by the "tracks" or train tracks (if they exist) between the White and Black sections of town. Metter was separated by the tracks that ran parallel to highway 46. Even if the tracks didn't physically exist, they were present in spirit and general understanding. Things have changed dramatically over time but in my early years most things were organized around those that were Black and those that were White.

One major change in my life was the transition from "Colored," to "Black" to "African American." The contents of this book are primarily focused on my early years. Given that context, I decided to use the term "Black" rather than African American to describe events in my early years as that was the terminology at the time. I will transition to the term African American later in the book as that is the more appropriate term today. I understand that decision might come with some controversy, but my attempt here is to communicate issues and thoughts that mostly focused upon my early personal life and how those events molded and shaped me. More importantly, the term Black was typically used at that time.

Today Metter is probably most known for being one of many counties in southeast GA that grow Vidalia onions. The Vidalia onion is a sweet onion due to low sulfur content in the soil of southeast GA. In my early years, Metter was probably most known for being the home of radio evangelist

Michael Guido. Michael Guido was a fixture on southern radio stations for his daily messages "A Seed from the Sower." Those messages were recorded in Metter and broadcast on radio stations across the southern US. He had a unique voice and he was a source of pride for many residents of Metter.

In my eyes, Metter was more than just the town of Metter and Candler county where I lived. To me, Metter was multiple locations including the neighboring towns of Cobbtown, Claxton, Reidsville and Statesboro; all of which were in close proximity to Metter. I had family and friends in each of those towns, so each seemed to be an extension of the "country" area where I lived.

My earliest family memories center around my uncle Roscoe, my grandmother Ellroe and my grandfather Curtis. I was raised mostly by my grandparents. When I was a small kid and I'm not sure what age, my mother had an opportunity to get a good job in New York. Since she was a single mother, she needed to consider taking the job to earn much needed money. Thus, my grandparents took on the task of raising me and my sister Mary. Although this arrangement wasn't supposed to be permanent, over time my mother married and had other children. Her life became settled in New York. At the same time, Mary and I had become fixtures in my grandparents' home. At some point, my grandmother decided we would not go to New York to live and would be raised in Georgia.

Some would wonder why a mother would leave her kids with her parents to take on a job so far away. But for me that wasn't that unusual. Blacks have always worked together and sometimes across generations to do what was best for all. Back in those days, it meant that the children may be left with a grandparent or an aunt or uncle to be raised while their parent made a living elsewhere. I have known sisters and brothers who have lived next door to one another while being raised by different family members. It was not as negative as it sounds because people had to go where they could make a living. That movement to make a living was typically the responsibility of the younger individuals in the family. I see a lot of beauty in that kind of arrangement as you have grandparents willing to raise their grandchildren to ensure that both their child and grandchildren had the best opportunities. Although my mom moved away, my sister and I were able to grow up in the same house and take care of one another. Even today we are still trying to take care of each other. Back then I remember just being a little kid with my sister and grandparents living in a little wooden house with them in the Charlton Grove community. Everything was good in my world.

Picture of my home in Charlton Grove

My first memory having anything to do with basketball was courtesy of my aunt Willa May who bought me my first basketball one Christmas. During Christmas, it was a custom of poor Black families in the South to "visit" and share food and stories with other family members. Some families were able to offer small presents. However, the purchase of a store-bought gift was a rarity. Aunt Willa May bought me one of those plastic basketballs and I remember just dribbling all around the house, or I guess trying to dribble it. I was probably six or seven years old at the time and that was my first basketball. I was amazed by the ball and I just dribbled and dribbled, but eventually I lost control of the ball, it rolled into the fireplace and burned up. My first basketball lasted just a few days.

My next memory having anything to do with basketball was when my uncle and grandad put a basketball goal outside our house. At that time, I wasn't a tall kid. The basketball goal was an inexpensive way to get me out of the house and to keep me busy. I was a short, fat and round kid about the same height as all of my friends. We used to play a lot of basketball in the yard and on sand. Yes, my first basketball experiences were on sand. Most kids grew up playing basketball on concrete, but we developed our early skills on sand in the yard. But even funnier was the guy who owned the house where we played basketball most of the time, was named "Sand." Sand was an older married guy who would play basketball with us to keep us out of trouble. To this day I don't know Sand's real name.

In order to get to each other's homes, we would walk or run on the interconnecting dirt roads in the Charlton Grove community. We might walk 3 to 4 miles a day on the dirt roads just to play ball. Sometimes we had short cuts through the woods that lessened the trip. That level of travel on foot was nothing for us at the time. We would play basketball or baseball all day and then we would walk back home at night. At the time, I was much better at baseball than basketball, and I considered myself as a really good hitter.

There was one common denominator among the kids in Charlton Grove; we were poor kids with no money. We didn't even think about money and

I'm not even sure we knew how poor we were. There is a saying that "Awareness is the beginning of change LaVon Mercer," so the change hadn't really begun because we had no awareness of the level of poverty that we were operating in. We were just poor kids enjoying our lives.

We used to play games in the woods where we jumped from tree to tree to see who was more agile or athletic. We didn't think about breaking our necks or having a serious injury. It was simply our goal to have fun. At other times we would play a more dangerous game involving a BB gun. During the game one of us would have a BB gun and the others would run around the woods trying to avoid being shot. Today it's crazy to think this was fun but we had no thoughts of having an eye injury and/or blindness. I would never let my kids have that kind of fun. Oftentimes we would leave the shooting game with a big bruise or a BB lodged in the skin. Another one of our hobbies was fishing. I still love to fish today. Some of my current fishing trips are designed to help me come closer to our heavenly Father and more importantly be willing to follow. I am called to be a fisher of men.

I remember having a cousin named "Daddy Pop" Lee Jones who lived in New York. Daddy Pop was my cousin so I'm not sure why we called him by that name. Daddy Pop left Dublin, GA which is about 45 minutes from Metter and moved to New York in the 1960s or 1970s. He had a great job with the Cadillac Company in New York and every year he used to always buy a new Cadillac. I wanted to grow up and be just like him. He was a very small guy, yet he always drove a big Cadillac. He looked odd riding in those big cars because of his small stature. He was in many ways a role model to me and his visits gave me something to look forward to and a person to aspire to be like.

Daddy Pop was an avid fisherman. Each time he came to GA he wanted to go fishing. So, we would go fishing in little ponds deep in the woods. Those fishing trips gave me an opportunity to discuss my life with him and hear about his adventurous life in New York. We would catch fish and clean them to cook. He worked so hard for Cadillac in New York that when he came south, all he wanted to do was just fish. He also loved eating GA grown peanuts. So, my grandmother always had peanuts for him.

Daddy Pop was one of the first people to explain to me that "money can't make you happy." He made a lot of money with the Cadillac corporation. He said over and over that money can't make you happy so find non-monetary ways to enjoy life. Daddy Pop's visits brought me great joy. Unfortunately, he died in car accident as a young man and I remember going to his funeral in New York. Despite his death, going to New York was the highlight of my year. Other than those memories, life was just slow and uneventful.

I am proud of the Charlton Grove community and the kids I used to hang with. All of them have become very successful men. One of my friends became an engineer and several of the guys have had successful and decorated military careers. The Charlton Grove community taught us to "believe is to commit to" and if you integrate those concepts into your day to day operation while learning to be punctual, diligent and loyal you will be successful. We also learned that we must have a great attitude and a willingness to sacrifice for others. Finally, we learned that we all must have a willingness to follow at times and most of all refuse to QUIT!"

RAPID GROWTH

"I have discovered in life that there are ways of getting almost everywhere you want to go, if you really want to."

Langston Hughes

GOD HAS A PLAN FOR OUR LIVES

Life started to change for me when I started growing at a very fast rate. The rapid growth is where I got the nickname "Tree." In Metter and surrounding towns, people still call me Tree. But entering middle school I wasn't that tall and was certainly not the tallest kid in my grade. I was just another average kid who was teased a lot. I wasn't much of a fighter, so I found myself getting my butt beat almost every day. But in the 7th or 8th grade one of the teachers noticed me fighting and that I was mad all the time. She challenged me to stand up for myself. I decided to stand up for myself, but then she ended up disciplining me for fighting. I just couldn't understand where she was coming from or the lesson that was to be learned.

Life was quite confusing in middle school. This was a time when physical discipline or "paddling" was the norm in the schools. I recall a paddling from Mr. William E. George, for doing something very stupid. Mr. George was our assistant principal and a towering figure. He was a tall and athletic man with huge hands. He was a great man, an educator and competitor who was known to consistently beat kids in foot races even in his forties and fifties. Mr. George was the agriculture teacher, but he found time to teach boys important things like how to tie the single or double Winston necktie knot.

Because two of my friends and I had engaged in some bad behavior, we had to face Mr. George. We hadn't yet learned that "God sometimes has to deconstruct the body and mind before he can build you up." I vividly remember that event because Mr. George was talking and paddling me all at the same time. He offered some critically important words that challenged me to be a better person. I will not discuss what he said here, but I will say his words were instrumental in my development at the time. Those words have constantly served as a reminder to aspire for excellence regardless of the situation.

When I finished the Lillian Street School and prepared to enter Metter High School, I was still just a gangly little kid. But the summer between my 8th grade and 9th grade year, I grew four inches. I remember that my grandmother bought me some pants during the early summer because they were on sale. When school started, they were two inches too short. She had to buy me new clothes to start school because I had grown so much.

The summer before entering high school was an interesting time for another reason. My grandmother hired me out to pick tobacco. Back then tobacco was picked by hand and not with the machines that you see today. Smoking was very prevalent and many farms in the South grew tobacco along with cotton and soybeans. My summer job was to pick tobacco, string tobacco and hang the tobacco up in the barn. I almost cut my finger off that summer in that job. As one might expect, none of the money that I earned went to me; it all went to my grandmother. That money was needed because my grandparents were constantly buying me clothes and food. It was also at this time that my grandfather had a stroke. I quickly became the man of the house and was needed to step up in many ways.

My 9th grade year was when everything changed. Not only was I still growing at a fast rate, but the schools were being integrated. The year before I started 9th grade, desegregation began. People were fighting in the streets for all sorts of reasons. Some were for desegregation and some were against desegregation. Blacks were fighting to remain at the Lillian Street School and not go to the integrated school. Whites were fighting to stop the Blacks from coming to Metter High School. It was a very very confusing time for me. My first year of high school I didn't play basketball. I tried out for basketball in the 9th grade. Going into those tryouts, I really thought I knew basketball. But I was not fluid or coordinated enough to play basketball. I also quickly learned that even though I could jump and run, I didn't know the game. So, I didn't make the team. I also tried to play football that year, but I was just too tall, gangly and uncoordinated. That was also the year that the late Len West came to Metter High School to become the head varsity basketball and baseball coach. Coach West became an instrumental figure in my life and much more than a basketball coach. Although not successful in the 9th grade, someone told me I should try basketball again in the 10th grade because I played street ball all the time and I was so tall.

I vividly remember meeting with Coach West and Coach Lee Hill to tell them I wanted to play basketball during my 10th grade year. After tryouts, Coach West told me I wasn't good enough to play on the varsity team and I began playing on the junior varsity (9th-10th grade team). My first coach was Lee Hill, who challenged me to get the best out of my abilities for him and myself. Coach West seems to remember that junior varsity team different than I do. He recalled that we were a horrible team, but the truth is we won most of our games with Coach Hill making us do things that we had never seen done before. We became a fast-paced run and gun team. We had a very successful junior varsity season. My grandmother didn't want me to play because she had arranged for me to work after school. My grandmother was depending upon me to work after school to earn money to help the family. During this same year, my grandfather died due to the complications of his stroke. That was a difficult time for me.

Entering into the 11th grade, I was ready to try out for the varsity team again. That same year, my grandmother became very ill. Her illness was very difficult for me because she really needed me to work to help support the family. But I really wanted to play basketball. I was constantly torn and struggling with what I should do. I decided it was going to be basketball and I would just have to figure out how to help the family and maybe work more after basketball season.

I started pre-season practice to prepare for the upcoming season. I had a major problem in that I didn't have a ride to my house out to Charlton Grove after practice. But because I was committed to basketball, a game I was really starting to love, I had to walk home from practice each day. Our home in Charlton Grove was approximately 10-12 miles from the high school gym. But the long walks home did not deter me from playing basketball. I made the 10-12 mile walk home each day for 2-3 weeks before anyone even noticed. It was then that people around me started to notice how committed I was to play the game I loved. I didn't even tell my grandmother that I was playing or walking home after practice because I didn't want to upset her.

I started to make significant progress on the court as Coach West and Coach Hill helped me really understand the game. Also, the guys around me were really good players and they pushed me to be better. We could see that we would be an excellent team if I could continue to improve. We might even become dominant if I could improve on offense and anchor our defense. At this point, I still didn't see myself as a great talent. I was just one of many guys trying to fill a role on the team and play the game we loved.

THE SEASON

"There is no better lesson than adversity. Every defeat, every heartbreak, every loss, contains its own seed, its own lesson on how to improve your performance next time."

Malcolm X

MERCY DOES NOT GIVE US THE BAD THINGS WE JUSTLY DESERVE

The summer leading into my junior season, Coach West took us to a basketball camp at Florida State University in Tallahassee, FL. In a strange turn of events, the best returning White player from the previous season declined to join us at the camp. When he decided not to join the team, we became an all Black team heading off to camp at Florida State University. To my knowledge, there were no other all Black teams in the area. This was virtually unheard of in that part of the state at that time and so close to desegregation.

Some of the players on that team had never traveled out of the state of Georgia. Traveling to Tallahassee, Florida was a really big deal for us. The camp at Florida State University was very competitive and prepared us for the upcoming season. We gained significant confidence at that camp. Although our school and community didn't know anything about us as a team, we knew we had the talent to become a very good team. We really jelled as a team at the Florida State University camp and we were ready for the upcoming season.

When the team was introduced in a pre-season pep rally, the athletic director said that they weren't expecting much out of us. We had only one starter coming back and that was Bruce Collins. Even I was an afterthought because I played junior varsity the prior season. So, it's not like anyone expected that I would offer much to the team.

The season started with little fanfare and we won our first few games. After our first few wins, we were faced with some major controversy. One afternoon, the one White player from the previous season who declined to join us at the Florida State University camp or to start the season with us, showed up at practice with his father ready to rejoin the team. He and his father decided that since we had won a few games it would probably be ok for him to play with us. We were stunned to see him return and expect to be on the team.

Coach West was a great diplomat and a fair man. He decided there would be a vote to determine if the White player could return to the team. One must understand that at this point of the season and our young lives we had bonded as a group of young men and a team. So, we had a big decision to make and one that was even more complicated by the fact that there were 12 guys already on the team and there were only 12 uniforms.

Ultimately, in order for the White player to rejoin the team, that would mean one of the current players who had already been playing and dedicated to the team, would have to give up his uniform. He would then basically be off the team. We all knew that the bridge between knowledge and skill is practice, and the White player had not engaged in any practice with the team or shown any dedication or commitment to the team. He only seemed to be interested in returning to the team because we had won a few games and were getting some attention.

Coach West decided to handle the decision in a democratic fashion. He would have one vote, Bruce Collins and I who were co-captains would have one vote and the rest of the team had a vote. The team and Bruce and I all voted no. Because Coach was a fair and honest man, the decision had been made. His vote didn't matter at that point. This gave Coach West the unenviable task of communicating to the player and his father that he would not be returning to the team mid-season or play his senior season. That discussion did not go well and was filled with racial slurs and threats. It's an ugly incident that we will all remember for the rest of our lives and one that really bonded the team going forward. With that incident behind us, the season progressed extremely well.

1974-1975 Metter High Tigers

The 1974-75 season (my junior year) begin with a 48-point win over Portal a school about 12 miles from Metter. Keith Lanier led us in scoring with 27 points and I had 14 points, 20 rebounds and 12 blocked shots. Our second game of the season was a 59-55 overtime win over Toombs Central. In that game I had 23 points, 28 rebounds and 8 blocked shots. By Christmas we were 4-0 heading into the Metter-Portal Christmas Invitation tournament held in Metter. We won the tournament by beating Statesboro a much larger school for the championship. I led the team in scoring with 31 points and I had 32 rebounds. I started to have a better feel for the game and how to dominate offensively and defensively. We also started to notice that people from neighboring towns were coming to see this all Black team dominate the competition in the area. We were beating schools in our region of the same size and larger schools in the area and outside of our region. We also started to develop a large fan base in the area.

Early January we had a 10-0 record and the team began to dominate in all phases of the game. By mid-January we were ranked 4th in the state in Class B behind Woodbury (ranked #1), Webster County and Towns County. At this point in the season I was averaging 20.5 points and a staggering 22.6 rebounds. The team was starting to get attention from all around the state. We lost a game in January but eventually moved our record to 14-1 after a beatdown of Emmanuel County Institute 84-60 and a hard fought 46-45 win over Glennville. We then lost our second game of the season in a rematch with rival Jenkins County (65-64). The game was an upset loss as we had the game in hand, but we missed our last three shots. I set a school record in that game by grabbing 41 rebounds and blocking 16 shots. We rebounded by beating Lyons 75-64 in a game of very balanced scoring as I had 18 points, Billy Edwards had 18, my best friend Herman Thomas had 14, co-captain Bruce Collins had 12 and Keith Lanier had 11. We then beat Reidsville by 21 points (78-57), Toombs Central by 43 points (94-51) and Treutlen County by 5 points (68-63). Late in the season we almost loss to Savannah Country Day, an all White private school from Savannah. The referees deliberately tried to take the game away from us, but we were able to prevail 58-57. We finished the season 21-2 and 18-1 in region games. The highlights of our season were a 12-0 record at home, being ranked all season and Metter-Portal Christmas Invitational Tournament champions. We finished the season ranked #2 in the state in Class B. I finished the season averaging 20.1 points and 25.0 rebounds.

We won our region tournament with a 48-47 victory in the title game over Montgomery County. The region championship game was a total defensive struggle and I led the team with 16 points, 20 rebounds and 8 blocks. Both teams received a berth in the state tournament in Macon, GA. We had a great time in Macon. We won our first-round game 73-65 over Buford. That night, Coach West went out to dinner with his brother who was a guitarist in a very famous band. The team was left unsupervised at the hotel. Boys will be boys and we found ways to have a great time. Guys were moving from room to room and having parties. When we played the next day, we did not play well. We lost to Union (Leslie) 69-61 which ended our season. The irony of those state playoffs was that we were beat by Union who was then beat by the 1975 Class B eventual state champion Monticello High School. Class B schools were the smallest in the state, but they had great athletes like Monticello's star player Ulysses Norris. Ulysses later became my college roommate. Ulysses played tight end in the NFL for several years with the Detroit Lions and the Buffalo Bills. After returning home to Metter from the state tournament, we felt bad that we hadn't delivered for Coach West who had done so much and taken so much heat for us.

Coach West was an excellent basketball coach. He was a young coach who was very competitive and ambitious, and this showed through his players. I believe he gave us his confident spirit. He gave us the idea that we were winners and we were going to win no matter what. I might even say that he birthed us from little kids to being teammates and then to being guys that loved the game, loved our families and loved God. He was an extremely spiritual man. Interestingly, the week after our loss in the state tournament, our local weekly paper published an article comparing our team to the last region champion from the 1930's. The article almost exclusively focused on the 1930's White Metter Bulldog team. This slight was a good indication of how little some in the community thought of our team.

Despite the extreme pressure and criticism, all the guys on that team were trying to do the right thing. We all went to different churches in Metter and we believed God first, family and so forth. Even though we had a great season, most of us were sad for the rest of the year. That ended up being the best team I played on at Metter. I gained much notoriety after that season and everything started happening for me. I started traveling and getting on airplanes which was new for me.

Coach West and I started traveling together and having more one on one time because I was now a college recruit. We were traveling to basketball camps and he had coaches who were friends that wanted to see me. We would go to games to make connections with other coaches. For example, one day I got out of school and Coach West said we were going to Alabama. We flew to Alabama on a very small plane and watched Leon Douglas who was the star player at The University of Alabama. Very few people knew we were doing things like that. It was his goal to move on to the college ranks. He had hoped to become an assistant coach at whichever program I signed with but unfortunately that did not happen.

Coach West was a really interesting guy. I think he had been at Metter High School for one season prior to the 1974-75 season. He was a very young-looking man, and some thought he was a student. There are many other aspects to Coach West's tenure as a coach at Metter High School that few know. Many did not know that he was selling sodas, popcorn and anything else that he could during our games to help me with food and other needs. He would try to do anything he could to make sure I was taken care of.

The other very interesting aspect of that season was the total support by some and total lack of support by others. Many members of the community provided money and other kinds of support for our travel and team needs. Others were just opposed to an all Black team. One community member provided some monetary support for the team although she had little knowledge of the team. Once she learned more about the team, she made a comment that she wouldn't have given any money if she knew it was just a bunch of n------s. The season was extremely tough because of opposition from referees and fans because of our race. Referees would make terrible foul calls or walking calls. We just decided the only way to overcome the calls was to run the hell out of the other teams. Not only could our players really run, we also had a lot of good shooters. Cheating referees weren't enough to overcome that team. The fans of the opposition were just brutal. It was common to hear "shoot it n-----, shoot it n-----."

All of this was happening in the early seventies when race relations in the South were still tenuous. I have vivid memories of the problems that our team created for the community. Some in the community did not approve of us for a variety of reasons. Whereas the team consisted of all Black players, the cheering squad was almost all White. This made our travel very interesting because the players and cheerleaders would travel together. Coach West took a lot of heat for the makeup of the team and the safety concerns that many had related to the White cheerleaders traveling with the Black players. Again, he had some support for the team in the community, but many were just against what was occurring.

Even though I was having great success in basketball, all was not well at home. My grandmother died that same year and I was absolutely devastated especially on the heels of my grandfather dying just two years earlier. A decision had to be made about where my sister and I would stay now that we had no real guardians. Finally, the decision was made that we would go to New York and stay with my mom. But I did not want to leave Metter and move to New York. I wanted to continue to play basketball in Metter. Coach lobbied for me to stay. One option for me to stay in Georgia was to move in with my father Curly Byrd and his wife Jearlean. They already had two sons in the home, and they lived in a neighboring town which would mean I was not in Metter's school district. I did not want to change schools and play for another school. I only wanted to play for Metter High School and Coach West. At some point, several members of the Black community agreed to help me with a place to stay. The final decision was that my sister would move to New York, but I would stay in Metter.

My first caretaker was Mrs. Marjorie Horton along with her husband Charles Horton who were my cousins. Mrs. Horton was a teacher and the mother of four children. The Hortons did an excellent job and I'm thankful for the time I spent with them. Later that year a gentleman by the name of Elmer Collins who was an educator and principal offered me a place to stay. I guess Mrs. Horton knew that I was placing a strain on the family, so she asked Mr. Collins for assistance. He owned a house that truck drivers used for living short-term and other individuals also used the house when they needed a place to stay. He agreed that I could stay in the house and he also agreed to help me get a job. The truck drivers lived in the back of the house and I lived in the front.

The living situation was crazy and fun all at the same time. The truck drivers had their girlfriends constantly coming in and out of the house. I became a gopher for the truck drivers for alcohol, food and anything else they needed. They would provide me with the money for the purchases and anything left over was my payment.

At the time, my best friend and teammate was Herman Thomas. Herman mentioned to his mother my living situation and she decided that was not appropriate for a teenager. Ms. Sarah Thomas (Momma Sarah) became my surrogate parent and I lived with them until my high school graduation. Her decision to allow me to live with them had a dramatic and positive effect on me. That decision has had a lasting impact on my life.

Momma Sarah was a very hard-working single mother of Herman and his four siblings Virginia, Diane, Wilfred and Michaela or Michelle as we always called her. Both Virginia and Diane had already left home. Diane was in the military which is something you didn't see often from women at the time and especially Black women. She was able to do that because she had a lot of toughness and inner strength. I always admired that about her. She was a lot like Momma Sarah in that way. Frankly, all of Momma Sarah's kids were like that.

Now looking back and having an adult perspective, that was probably not the best decision for Momma Sarah or her family. Herman was senior when I moved in, Wilfred was in middle school I believe, and Michelle was in elementary school. It's funny to think back and remember that Michelle served as the pre-game hair stylist for Herman and me, as well as other guys on the team. Although she was just in elementary school, she made sure our afros were picked out just right or she braided our hair in cornrows just like NBA star Kawhi Leonard wears today. Think about that, we had a little girl doing a job that adults now get paid to do today and make a lot of money. A lot of NBA players have a team of people working for them today and almost always on that team is a barber or hair stylist if they have long hair.

So, Momma Sarah had a lot of mouths to feed. Years earlier her husband had been murdered. She was a single woman raising me and three other children. Yet because she was a very no-nonsense type of woman, that tragic event was not going to define her or stop her from achieving the goals she set for her family. She seemed to work day and night to take care of us. Momma Sarah also found ways for us to make money as teenagers including cleaning churches and working with her at Junior's Supper Club where she worked part-time as a cook. One benefit of that job was us being able to eat steaks. WOW!

But let's be clear, Momma Sarah took care of everybody. We were kids and I'm not sure I really understood the extreme pressure she was under because she never complained. When I was added to the family, that increased her burden. Despite that pressure, I never felt any sense of burden from her. My junior year I believe I had reached 6'-8" or 6'-9." At that height, purchases like a suit or tuxedo virtually impossible. Yet Coach West and Momma Sarah bought me a light blue tuxedo to make sure I could experience the prom. So today when I see coaches making millions of dollars but players struggling, I think of all that they did for me.

I don't know that I remember all of Momma Sarah's jobs, but I do recall I learned my work ethic and perseverance from her. She made a lot of her income as a seamstress. She had a little shop in downtown Metter, and she did a lot of sewing at home. She could make anything. If you could envision it, she could make it. In another time period she probably would have been a famous fashion designer. She made clothes for me and even made me a suit once. It was just nothing for her to do that. She told me to stand up straight and stand still and she made a few measurements. A few days later the suit was finished. It's pretty shocking now to think that a person could create a suit for someone almost seven feet tall without a team of people. She just had an eye for how to make things and an amazing sense of fashion. When she got dressed for church or any meetings that she had to attend, her suit, shoe and purse combinations were always perfectly coordinated. We might have been poor, but she did not accept us coming out of that house without looking the best that we could.

She was also an interior decorator. She had a unique perspective on how things should look. She could walk into any house and within minutes tell you what needed to be rearranged or what color scheme was needed. It's just a reminder that talented strong-minded people can and will do whatever they have to do to get the job done. They are also the kind of people who will accomplish whatever goals they set for themselves. When I played, I would call on that attitude when games got tight or when I was battling it out with some of the great big men of the game. Whether playing in the rugged Southeastern Conference (SEC) or the Israeli leagues I felt I could always dig a level deeper than my opponent because of learning that toughness from her. I would never quit until I was out of the game or the last whistle was blown.

Momma Sarah owned a brick house on Lillian street which was the center of the Black community. Her house was less than a mile from where the Lillian Street School was located. I emphasize "brick" because it was a big deal to own a brick house back then. Few Black people that I knew owned them. For me, that house was awesome and a major upgrade from where I was living. Most importantly there was a lot of love in that house. The house had three bedrooms, one bathroom and was probably less than 1000 square feet. If you came into the room where I slept, you would see my feet hanging off the bed because there were no beds long enough for my tall frame. But we were all in the house, warm when we needed to be, cool when we needed to be and always fed and clothed.

Momma Sarah was a feisty woman who wouldn't put up with any crap from us. But she always started her interactions with love and service to us all. When people ask me what the Thomas family means to me I simply say, everything.............they are my family.......period. They are my brothers and sisters and we came up as one unit. We learned to fight together and cover each other's backs when that was necessary, or stuff was going on. I would not be where I am today if it wasn't for them.

GETTING NOTICED AND RECRUITMENT

"Challenges make you discover things about yourself that you never really knew."

Cicely Tyson

NEVER CONFUSE YOUR SELF WORTH WITH YOUR NET WORTH

My senior year we were rebuilding but we still had a good team. But the team had changed drastically. Herman and many of my close friends graduated at the end of my 11th grade year. From that team Herman Thomas, Bruce Collins, Gabriel Summerlin, Larry Hobbs and Keith Lanier were all gone. The only guys left from that team were Billy Earl Edwards and Stacey Whitaker. My senior year I spent most of my time with Billy Earl. Even though Herman went off to college, I continued to stay with Momma Sarah and the family.

All of the players were committed to going to camps and improving their skills. I remember going to a camp at Stetson University in Deland, Florida where I met the late Darryl Dawkins aka "Chocolate Thunder." Darryl was a man child who went directly from high school to the NBA. Darryl wasn't a camp attendee, but he was in the area to watch some games. Darryl was the biggest man I had ever seen. Over time I became good friends with Darryl and learned that he was one of the nicest people and one of the biggest teddy bears in the game.

The camp in Deland was probably one of the first times I had to face a true challenge on the basketball court. There were players attending the camp that knew the game better than I did. I realized very quickly that I needed to improve dramatically. I remember that I was getting dominated early in the camp and a coach at the camp Glenn Wilkes pulled me to the side and said "LaVon, you're doubting yourself. You're better than most of the players here. Why don't you just go out and relax and play? Don't worry about the game, just play the game." From then on, I started having one of my best camps and my stock went from a virtually unknown player out of Metter, to a big fish in a big lake. That's one of the reasons I don't doubt myself in life today because of people like Coach West, Coach Hill, Coach Wilkes and Momma Sarah.

Suddenly, all the scouts started looking at me as a future Division I player. From that point, they started recruiting me really hard to come to their schools. My confidence rose drastically, and I came into my senior year ready to dominate. Even though everything looked great for me, it was a very trying year. Much of the difficulty centered on Herman leaving for college and I no longer had my close friend. I really depended on him a lot as a good friend and buddy. While I was struggling with that loss, everybody in the country started recruiting me and I no longer had that old team for support.

Coach West had a box in his office that was about three feet tall and two feet wide. He would get a stack of mail for me in his office each day. We would look at the mail and since I had an idea of the schools that I was interested in, he would tell me if any of those schools sent letters. He would take letters from the schools that I had an interest in and put those on the edge of his desk so that I could read them. All the others went into the box. I just tried to focus on playing basketball. I really didn't want to get involved with being recruited and trying to play basketball at the same time. It was just one year after my grandmother's death, so I just didn't have the kind of energy and focus necessary for the recruiting process.

Momma Sarah arranged for me to do odd jobs and earn money. This was an opportunity for me to get away from the recruiting process. Because Herman was away at college, I would do some of the work with his younger brother Wilfred. On one job, I washed dishes at a little chicken restaurant. There were many others and each one gave me a reprieve from the recruiting process. In some ways, this was a fun time. It seemed that you had nothing, but at the same time you had everything. I felt loved, had people around me and all my needs were being met.

Metter wasn't much in to basketball at first and didn't care if we were winning. Metter and most of southeast Georgia is all about football. That was until Oral Roberts came to Metter. Oral Roberts was a well-known television-evangelist and was one of the most recognized Christian ministers worldwide at the time. He founded Oral Roberts University in Tulsa, OK in 1963 based on what he says was a command from God. If you went to Oral Roberts University as a student, you agreed to sign an honor code document which was a pledge to not engage in drinking, smoking or premarital sex.

Somehow word got out that Oral Roberts himself was coming to see us play. That created a major stir in our little town. Usually in order to get into our games you had to arrive at the gym before the start of varsity girl's game. When word got out that Oral Roberts was in town and coming to the game, people were standing outside the gym two to three hours before the girl's game. People that I never knew lived in Metter were standing in line just to see Oral Roberts. My guess is that most were not really interested in seeing us play and they were only interested in seeing Oral Roberts. But because they were not our regular fans, they didn't know that the regular fans had already received their tickets before the game. And for the others, if you got there early you got in and if you didn't arrive early you didn't get in.

Honestly, I didn't even know who Oral Roberts was at the time. I'm not sure that I watched enough TV to know who he was. I certainly wasn't spending a lot of time watching a TV evangelist. Besides, Metter had Michael Guido who was spreading the gospel with his radio evangelist messages. In our minds, he was really famous because he was on the national radio. His studio is a half a mile from Momma Sarah's house and if you ran fast, you could probably be there in less than five minutes. I didn't give much thought to Oral Roberts coming to the game because I wasn't going to Tulsa Oklahoma; wherever that was. I was just a country kid trying to play basketball because the game gave me peace. I didn't have to worry about my grandparents being sick again. Basketball was a way to get away from people.

There were so many people (fans, coaches, etc.) at our games that I didn't know who was in attendance. Hugh Durham who was the head coach at Florida State University at the time attended some of the games and I never knew it. Representatives from The University of Georgia used to rent vans and drive three hours down from Athens, GA to see me play. I had some disappointing times that year because I really didn't know what I was getting into with the recruiting process. I just wanted to be a kid playing basketball and ignore everything else. I never wanted the fanfare or to feel like I was better than anyone else. But I did get to meet people like Coach John Thompson at Georgetown University. I didn't know who he was or anything about Georgetown. In fact, I knew very little about Washington, DC so Georgetown did not make my list of schools of interest. Later in life, I got to know Coach Thompson and he has been one of my best mentors.

My senior year I averaged 37.6 points, 30.1 rebounds and 12 blocks. I've been asked, many times how do you average 30 rebounds in a 32-minute high school game? My answer is I was quick and I out hustled people. And it didn't hurt that I was 6'-10" and taller than most of the competition. But there are shorter players who are great rebounders. I always admired Dennis Rodman for his rebounding prowess, and he was only 6'7." Rebounding is not just grabbing the ball. Sometimes you have to hit it against the backboard and go get it.

A writer from the Atlanta Journal and Constitution challenged Coach West on his rebounding counts. Actually, Coach West didn't count rebounds or points or anything; he had someone else in the program to do that. Coach West sent a tape of the game to the writer and told him to count them for himself. When he contacted Coach again, he said "You were wrong, you missed one."

Small schools like Metter have always had good ball players and great athletes. But because football is king in the state of GA, they often got overlooked. In basketball if you win a couple of games then great, but the concentration is on football. Everybody wants a Herschel Walker, the Heisman Trophy winner from The University of GA.

A great Metter player that I remember and regret not being able to play with was a guy named Dennis Murphy. Dennis and I never played together but we used to play in the gym and in the park. It used to be fun because we used to go at it. I really wished Coach West would have stayed in Metter. Dennis was the kind of talent that had the attitude that I think would have made it to the pros. He just had so much talent and he could jump.

Dennis was like many of the great players I played with over the years. He understood the game. Most great players will tell you the game is not played at the moment. Great players can tell you what you're going to do before you do it. They're already anticipating what you're going to do. When you get to a certain age and you've had enough coaching, then you learn to anticipate what your opponent is going to do. For some you might need to simply set them up so that you can either block their shot or get the rebound. And that's the way the game is truly played. The best guys that I've ever played with or played against all had one thing in common, they thought out the game two steps ahead of most other players.

Dennis was one of the first players to come down south from New York to Metter. Dennis was a great ball handler and he could really play. I believe my senior year he was in the 10th grade, but coach wouldn't play him on the varsity. I thought they should have brought him up my senior year because I believed he was going to be the greatest thing going. At the time, he was around 6'1" but he grew to 6'5" or 6'6" and ended up playing at Georgia Southern College (now Georgia Southern University) which is about 15 miles from Metter. He was on the first team from Georgia Southern to ever make the NCAA tournament. In 1981 Dennis' younger brother Caradio led Metter to the state championship final game. Metter lost by one point following a controversial foul call and tip in at the buzzer. They finished their season Class A state runner-up. Although Metter has never won a state title, a lot of talented players have played at Metter High School.

I was just one of many very good ball players from Metter. Unfortunately, my senior season ended with an early playoff loss in a region game. We did not return to the state playoffs as expected. Just like that, it was all over for me and high school basketball. In my two varsity seasons, I was named my region's most valuable player and to the all-state basketball team each season. I was named the Georgia High School Association Player of the Year for the 1975-1976 season and a high school All-American. Little did I know that everything was about to change in my life and in ways that I could never have imagined. Playing basketball just for fun was all over.

THE DIFFICULTY OF THE DECISION

"Nothing in life that's worth anything is easy."

Barack Obama

High school in general was a confusing time. Although I was known as LaVon the basketball star, there was also LaVon the student. Several of the Black teachers at Metter High School were family members and they looked beyond basketball at the bigger educational picture. They saw Black students as a representative of their families, and they wouldn't tolerate you embarrassing the family. For them your education was personal and a source of pride. So, they operated with one goal in mind and that was success or as we used to say, "no half-stepping." They regularly told me that I was going to learn more than just basketball and that included Math, English and other subjects that many high school kids cared little about. Mrs. Hodges was one of my Math teachers and she made it known to me that I was going to learn every aspect of Math and at least on par with every other student in the grade. She did not cut me any slack. I had to learn all kinds of formulas and focus on exactly what she said I needed to learn. She was on me twenty-four seven and for that I am very appreciative.

I also had Mrs. Horton, who was also an excellent teacher who became one of my caretakers. She was also a guidance counselor. She didn't play around and didn't care how big a basketball star I was. She stayed on my butt to make sure I did everything I needed to do to make it to the next level. Mrs. Horton lived next door to Momma Sarah, so she was on Herman as well. She encouraged us to think outside of basketball. Mrs. Dot Campbell was another person who checked on me even in college. Her primary interest was in my grades. Even after I entered college, she would set up appointments with my advisor to check on my grades. She made them pull my grades so she could see what I was doing. My development was important to her because the word among some in Metter was don't worry, he'll be back in Metter soon because he's not that smart and he's not college material. Oftentimes these comments came from people right in the Black community who claimed to care about me. Mrs. Campbell used to always tell me "LaVon you're gonna make it and I'm gonna make sure you do what you have to do." She was a relative of mine, so it was very personal to her. She wanted me to know the family was depending on me to lead in that area. I thought I was just playing ball and I didn't even understand the significance of it all.

I also had White teachers that were just as concerned about my education. I had this short tiny English teacher Mrs. Jessie Bird. We had to learn every part of speech and how to diagram long sentences in her class. We diagramed sentences for hours on end. She seemed to also get involved in my personal life and relationships in addition to academics. She would get in our face to get the academic outcome that she wanted. She was not afraid of students and took a very different approach to teaching than what we see today. We had our science teacher Mrs. Youmans who would laugh with us but at the end of the day we had better get the work completed. We were surrounded by strong teachers. And Coach West would make his rounds to all the teachers to see how his players were doing in class. It wasn't just about me, but everyone on the team. Coach West cared about the academics of all the players on the team. He also reached out to players at other high schools to help them move on to college and allow their basketball talents enhance their futures.

My senior year there were three guys that everybody in the country wanted. The three players were Reggie Johnson, Ricky Brown, and me. We were all high school All-Americans and top prospects. My first pick for college was Tennessee and everybody knew that. Reggie Johnson and I had become great friends after playing together at several camps. We played well together, and we made a pack to go to Tennessee together. The University of Georgia was in the picture as well. The University of Detroit where Dick Vitale was the coach was in the picture until I got off the plane in Detroit. It was so cold in Detroit and I made my decision at the airport that I would not go to Detroit for college. Kentucky was also in the mix because of their tradition. They had Rick Robey at the time, and he was a super player. If I had gone to Kentucky, there would have been two LaVons on the team. They already had a guy named LaVon Williams. And Florida State University was also in the mix. When the time came, I chose The University of Georgia (UGA). There was a lot of pressure for me to stay in the state of Georgia and go to my state school.

The recruiting process that ultimately led to me signing with UGA was absolutely terrible. It was at times somewhat fun in that so many schools wanted me. But the recruiting process had a dirty underbelly that those not directly involved couldn't see. I had over 300 schools interested in me and some would go to great lengths to try to get me to sign. At the same time, I would find ways to avoid schools and recruiters. UGA reported in a newspaper article that they had spent an entire day in Metter trying to see me, but they were never able to find me. Actually, the process got so frustrating that I took a complete hiatus from it all including Coach West. I felt pressure from every angle, and it was unclear who had my best interests in mind. Few people remember that I signed with Georgia Southern College (GSC) just two days after I signed with UGA. The coach at GSC was a good friend of

Coach West and I thought that might be a better option than UGA. I told Coach West that I didn't think UGA had the tradition or national rankings. I didn't feel like I would fit into their program. But I knew I wasn't really going to GSC because they had a terrible floor in their gym that was bad on your knees. After signing with GSC, I found out there was an NCAA rule that if you signed with a Division I school, you couldn't then sign with a school in a lower division. At the time GSC was Division IAA. Coach West was also taking a lot of heat for my decisions and people were saying a lot of inpugnating things about him especially the people at UGA. But he said over and over, he just wanted to help me do what I wanted to do. Coach West went so far as to publicly accuse the UGA Athletic Board of using "pressure tactics" to get me to sign. At some point in the process, UGA had used up their maximum visits allowed by the NCAA and could only use telephone calls. Even though they could no longer visit, it didn't mean they couldn't make contact. I don't know if that was better or worse. Ultimately, I decided to go to UGA which was close to home and allowed me to play in the Southeastern Conference (SEC).

MOVING ON

"I have learned that success is to be measured not so much by the position that one has reached in life as by the obstacles which he has to overcome while trying to succeed."

Booker T. Washington

DO NOT GIVE UP ON YOUR HARVEST, THE SICKLE WILL BE SHARP

In the fall of 1976, I headed to The University of Georgia (UGA) to start the second phase of my basketball journey. UGA is in northeast GA in the city of Athens. Athens is a little over an hour's drive from Atlanta the capital city of Georgia. UGA has a very beautiful campus with the landmark black arches on the northern end of the campus on Broad Street. The state of Georgia was the first state to charter a state supported university in 1784 when they set aside 40,000 acres of land for the school. Because UGA did not start admitting students until 1801, the University of North Carolina at Chapel Hill makes the claim of being the oldest university. They started admitting students in 1795. Regardless, I have visited each campus, and both are beautiful and immaculate places of higher learning.

College was tough and the transition from a school of less than 400 students to a major university is something that is very hard to describe. I enrolled in classes that had more students than my entire senior class at Metter High School. Herman and then much later Michelle had the same experiences at UGA. If you went to a small high school, it may be difficult for you to imagine sitting in a freshman class and in a lecture hall with almost as many students as were in your entire high school. Even though I was up to the challenge, it became obvious very quickly that the education you receive at small-town rural school is very different than what kids receive at larger schools in cities like Atlanta. Now don't get me wrong, I received an excellent and quality education at Metter High School. But the resources that larger school districts in cities like Atlanta have, allow them to offer more advanced classes to their students. Consequently, students from larger schools may come to the university having taken classes in subjects like Calculus or Microbiology when the most advances classes at small schools like Metter would have been Precalculus or general Biology. It's simply the difference between the haves and have nots when it comes to what can be offered to students.

I had traveled quite a bit during the basketball recruitment process, but there were still things about the university campus and Athens that were novel. The campus had a bus system just for students and faculty. The buses traveled a north-south route and an east-west route. Because of the size of the campus, you couldn't simply walk from class to class if they were back to back and on the opposite ends of the campus. That was a new concept for me. It was always interesting to be on those busses at 6'10". It was hard not to be noticed and recognized as a basketball player.

I was at UGA to play basketball, but I understood football was king just as it is all over the state of Georgia. The biggest reminder is right in the middle of campus; Sanford Stadium. Sandford Stadium is one of the largest college football stadiums in the country. Legendary Coach Vince Dooley was at the helm of the Bulldog football program when I arrived. Ironically in the Fall of 1980 and right after I left UGA, Coach Dooley lead the team to a national championship behind the running of Hershel Walker. Walker grew up in Wrightsville, GA which is one hour from Metter. He went to a very small school just like Metter High School.

Our home basketball games were played at the Coliseum. It was renamed the Stegeman Coliseum in 1996. The Coliseum was first opened in 1964 and has about 10,000 seats. College basketball is nothing like high school in that there is no off-season. In high school you just play for fun and after the season is over you play in parks or anywhere else you can find. And if you don't want to play in the off-season, then you just don't.

In college, it's a constant process of trying to get better. Parts of the process are not formal or led by coaches, but someone is always watching or monitoring to see what you are doing. Also, in college, everyone on the team is a really good player. Not all players have the same strengths, but they are good at something and that is the reason they were offered a scholarship. Each player on the team was the best player on his high school team and likely the best player in his area or part of the state. That fact brings a lot of egos to the team which must be molded into one unit.

My freshman year I played all 27 games and averaged 12.0 points and 7.6 rebounds. We had a terrible season winning only nine games and three of our 18 conference (SEC) games. Although I had a good freshman season, life outside of basketball at UGA was difficult. UGA like many Division I schools, had classes designed mostly to keep players eligible to play rather than a true commitment to learning. I distinctly remember the first day of my first English class when the professor came in and said, "If you are Black or you're an athlete, then you don't need to be in my class." I took heed to that warning and dropped the class immediately.

My first year at UGA there were about 900 Black students on campus. The total enrollment was almost 24,000. If I had a class with another Black student, it was a total phenomenon. After the first year, I learned to try to find people who were in the same major or had the same interests. That way you could take the class with them and have someone to study with. If you did not, you were sort of lost and had no one to lean on for support. At the time, students didn't share notes unless you were in a White fraternity where they had years of notes, copies of old tests and everything you needed to pass a class. Most professors back then didn't change much about their classes or tests, so notes and previous tests were readily available to fraternity members. These experiences forced Black students to stay connected. I'm still connected to many Black and White students who went to UGA with me.

There were a group of Black professors who lived in Athens who served as surrogate parents for us. They knew we were in Athens without the

support of our families and frequently isolated. They would invite us into their homes for dinners and other events to offer us support. Many of them later became friends and I still see them from time to time. They did a lot to save us from flunking out and worked to make our experience tolerable. Now please don't think I did not enjoy my UGA experience; I am a Bulldog for LIFE and LOVE IT!

There was another interesting and very nice lady that I met at UGA by the name of Dr. Jan Kemp. Dr. Kemp started following the academic progress of athletes and completing research on their progress. She was especially interested in student athletes who were enrolled in remedial classes. She asked me one time "Why are you in this class?" I said to her, "They gave me this schedule" and so forth. She then said, "You don't need to be in this class." In 1981, Dr. Kemp accused and complained to UGA administrators that the football coaches intervened to allow nine players pass a remedial English course. This allowed them to play in the 1981 Sugar Bowl. In 1982 she was demoted and eventually dismissed from the university. She sued UGA because she felt she was dismissed because of her complaints. She eventually won a judgement for

$2.5 million dollars and was reinstated to the university. The judgement was later reduced to $1.08 million and the university president resigned shortly afterwards. Dr. Kemp remained in Athens even after retiring from UGA. She died in 2008 due to complications associated with dementia.

I enjoyed playing basketball at UGA, but most of the time we just didn't have it together. I especially enjoyed playing in the SEC because of the strong competition. The team was very inconsistent during my time there and the only time the team would play was when we were pissed off. I remember one year we went to a Christmas tournament I believe my sophomore year. In the tournament was Ohio State and Louisville. Louisville had Darrell Griffith or "Mr. Dunkenstein" for his vicious dunks and Ohio State had 6'11" Herb Williams who was later a first-round pick in the 1981 NBA draft. Louisville was ranked #7 at the time and Ohio State had what most considered the best recruiting class in the nation with Herb Williams. We were having a team dinner and the Ohio State players were talking loud and cracking jokes about how they were going to beat us the next day. I remember my teammate Lucius Foster saying "Tree, Tree we going to mess them up tomorrow." Lew who was also 6'10" couldn't be stopped when he was pissed off. We discussed the dinner later that night and everyone was challenged to bring their "A" game.

We had an assistant Coach Calvin Jones who met with us before the game. He stepped away from Coach John Guthrie our head coach and huddled us up on the court. He said some words I will never forget. He said, "Look guys, let me tell ya'll something. They don't think we can play. All that other stuff that we are supposed to be doing, forget that. I want you guys to run pick and roll all game and you boys play the way I know that you guys can play." Coach used a lot more profanity than I can include here, but the message was very clear.

This thought process contrasted with Coach Guthrie who had the mentality that whoever won the NBA championship then that's the offense he tried to install for that season. All of my other coaches had their own philosophies. You must have your own system and then bring in players to fit your system. He just brought in a bunch of great talent, but he had no system. When I was there, he had the most talent UGA probably ever had on a basketball floor. He had no system and he didn't recruit players for whatever system he was trying to run.

So, the game tipped off and we start balling. We played Ohio State first and it was expected they would beat us and play Louisville for the championship. We started rolling and we beat Ohio State 84-80. My stat line was 29 points, 17 rebounds and 7 blocks in the game against Ohio State while Herb Williams had 22 points, 9 rebounds and 3 blocks. The next night it was UGA vs Louisville and we beat them too 73-70. Lew, Walter Daniels and I were on the all-tournament team. SportsCenter did a little special on us and said UGA might be a team that could make some noise and upset some people. After the tournament we went home for Christmas break.

After the Christmas break, we came back, and we were thinking that the coach would now let us play and we were ready to go. Coach Guthrie came into practice and kicked a basketball as hard as he could. The ball went off a teammate Curtis Jackson's head and into the upper stands. He started

cursing and yelling "you didn't run my offense.......you didn't do this.....
you didn't do that." We were all just thinking man don't you realize we just
beat two of the best teams in the country. Yeah, we didn't run your offense
because your offense sucks and does not fit our talent. We probably went
on an eight or nine game losing streak after that.

Guys were upset and some were discussing transferring. Coach Guthrie
was fired at the end of the year. There was a lot of losing in the men's
programs while I was at UGA. The coaching staff seemed to always make
excuses for our losing rather than take some of the blame for poor coaching.
In the papers he would say one week that we were inexperienced. The next
week he would say we weren't running the offense smoothly or not
rebounding enough. There were always excuses to explain our losing and
true enough some of the mistakes were a function of me and my teammates
poor play. But that's why you have a coaching staff to eliminate those kinds
of problems.

My junior year Coach Hugh Durham came to UGA from Florida State
University and we started winning a little more. My junior season we were
14-14, and I lead the team in scoring at 14.4 ppg. and rebounding at 7.7 rpg.
My senior season he brought in Terry Fair, future NBA Hall of Famer

Dominique Wilkins and some other really good players. We ended the season 14-13 and after that my time at UGA was over. I ended my career with an average of 11.6 points and 7.8 rebounds. I hold the UGA record for most blocks in a career with 302, career field goal percentage at 60.2% and best single season field goal percentage at 64.2%. Three seasons after I left UGA they made it to the Final Four, losing to the eventual national champion North Carolina State 67-60.

A NEW JOURNEY

"It isn't where you come from; it's where you're going that counts."

Ella Fitzgerald

MAN WITHOUT VISION FOR HIS FUTURE WILL RETURN TO HIS PAST

There are major changes in what is expected of you on the basketball court when you go from high school to college and from college to professional basketball. In high school, it's fun, family and friends. In college, you learn quickly that your performance is probably helping pay for one, two, three or possibly four coach's kids to go to private high school or their college tuition. You are also putting food on the coach's table and making sure his wife has new shoes.

When you move to professional basketball, you forget about all the college coaches and people in high school. You must make sure you keep a job. The game is now a business for you. Now you must make sure you have shoes, clothes, a house and automobiles for you and your family. At this point everyone is counting on you for everything. It creates a different priority when you're going to practice. Practice in high school was just fun and you spend your time trying to see who could shoot better or whatever. College is different because you are prepping for a professional basketball career even though you seem to be just playing to pay for a coach's Mercedes or whatever else was required for his family. When you get to the professional level, it is strictly about you. With the additional monies you can help other people but, in all honesty, you must learn to take care of yourself first. Interestingly, there was probably more pressure placed on me in college. Once you get to the pros and are getting a paycheck, it doesn't feel like much pressure. It is now your duty to perform which is something different. You must improve your skill level just to stay in the game. So, most players do the exact same things to stay in the game.

In 1980, I went to play in Italy in a summer league to get ready for the upcoming NBA draft. I lived in the city of Pesaro which is on the Adriatic coast in the northeast portion of Italy. Pesaro had a population of around 90,000 at that time. I wanted to play ball and stay in shape, so I decided to go to Italy to play. It was at this point that basketball changed for me, because now I was starting to get paid to play. It wasn't a lot of money but every two weeks I was receiving two to three thousand dollars. I thought that was pretty cool.

Italy is a great place. There were a lot of American players in Italy when I played there. Some of them have never moved back to the US. They haven't abandoned their families in the US, but they decided to live there permanently. They have nice jobs and they seem to be doing exactly what they want to do. They generally don't come back to the US. They will come back if something happens in the family to visit for a few weeks. But after a few weeks back, they generally cannot adjust to the US and decide to return home. I went to Italy with the understanding that I would get to play against some great players and prepare for the NBA.

At the end of the Italian summer league, I knew that I would either play another year in Italy or Europe somewhere or just go back to the US for the NBA draft. Italy or any other European team would be a great opportunity because if I didn't make it in the NBA I could possibly be picked up by other teams. When I flew to Italy to play, I received my first passport. I traveled a lot on that passport. If I held it up from the dinner table, it would touch the floor. The US government had to constantly extend my passport because of my frequent travel.

When I arrived in Italy, the car of choice back then was the Fiat. We drove to the city and they checked me into a small hotel. The hotel was owned by the same person who owned the team. I started to meet a lot of people. They would take me around to see the sights in the city. Now at that time I was still thinking that I was having fun, and this was just basketball. I met some of the most beautiful women in the world in Italy. The whole scene in Italy was like a big party. We had a guy on the team that we used to call "pretty boy." Pretty Boy was the only person who would speak a little English and a little Italian. We would have conversations of broken Italian and English. He was the guy who would tell us what the coach was saying and help us find places to go to dinner.

I learned quickly that when you go to Europe to play, you are just a product. For example, if a group of Italians start selling pasta in the US and the pasta is not good, then Americans will go somewhere else to get pasta. Basketball was just like that. If they didn't like your services as a player, they would move on to find another player. But most of the guys didn't understand that's how it worked. Initially I had that kind of thought process until I met some of the players who had been there for a while. Those players helped me to understand and adjust to being a professional athlete.

You must understand that you're just a PRODUCT and you're only as good as your last game. If you don't perform, you will be on a plane home. You might think you're going to practice the next day, but they will have you on a plane going home. You must learn to always monitor what you're doing. We didn't eat or drink with the team coaches or trainers because we didn't know who was going back to tell management about our actions. You also didn't go out with too many of the women, because you didn't know if they were going back to the management to report your activity. You were there on the team, but you had to be careful about what you were doing during your off time.

Early on there, I met a guy named Wilbur Holland. Wilbur was always trying to help me understand the business. Wilbur would say, "LaVon you are still thinking about this as a game; basketball is a business." "You are a product, don't think that you are not a product." The first thing he taught me is you're only as good as your last game. You can see that mentality in games today. Guys will play the whole game and in the last quarter, they will try to pad their numbers. They will try to get every rebound they can. They will try to score as many points as possible. The only thing they are doing is padding their numbers. But it doesn't change the fact that they still sucked the entire game. But at the end of the game, when you look at their stat sheet (which most people do today), it looks like they had a great game. Wow; he had 30 points. But he sucked as a player because he destroyed the rest of the team chemistry. Today, basketball is very individualized instead of a sport that is about the team. These days there are just a few teams that play together as one unit.

The beauty of basketball was always the team. The team effort; the team wins. Everybody loves LeBron. I'm ok with the fact that LeBron changed teams to win a championship. And there is nothing wrong with that. One team, two teams maybe. But changing teams, multiple times just to get to win a championship is ridiculous. Players should always ask themselves did I help build a team or just use the team to get what I wanted? Because there is beauty in staying to build a team. That's why you can't compare an Oscar Robertson or some of the guys back then to the guys of today. Those older players were drafted by a team and most of the guys would retire there. They would stay there and build the team not always by choice because the rules were different then. Most of the guys today are just jumping from team to team to team even if they are not cut by the team. I always wonder if all that jumping from team to team helps them win more championships.

Basketball in Italy in some ways was similar to the US and in other ways very different. One of the biggest differences in the game had to do with running the fast break. For example, in the US running the fast break was to score a layup. In Europe you ran the fast break for the jump shot or the "Three Pointer." A lot of those differences about the game were based on how the lane was shaped. The lane was wider down low and the basic moves that we were taught in high school or college wouldn't work. Big men and low post players had to learn to add a dribble to account for the difference. You had to learn new moves because the lane was wider. Moves that you used like the one dribble bounce had to be changed. You might have to use a drop step, dribble and then go. You had to practice those new moves over and over until they were smooth and efficient. It probably took me until midseason of the first year to feel comfortable with the change in play.

Also, in Europe, big guys had to learn to shoot and not just sit in the paint (which is in the lane) the way they used to do when I played. Most of us were taught to use the glass to shoot the ball. We had a lot of jump shooting drills to improve that aspect of our game. It wasn't an easy process. I was taught by a European coach that with every move I made, I should have three options. You had your base move and if you tried to cut me off, I had three different things I could do to score. His additional input and information made my career last a great deal longer. So, it's not really like you could stop anybody there that easily. As a player you had to make a lot of moves to stay in the game.

You also had to learn to pass. There was a gentleman named Neal Walk who was one of the first post players that I saw who could really pass. Neal was the second pick after Lew Alcindor (who later became Kareem Abdul Jabbar) in the 1969 NBA draft. Neal played for the University of Florida in college and played for the New Orleans Jazz and the New York Knicks in the NBA. Neal and I had practices where we just worked on passing. I used to be afraid to let the ball just go on a pass. Neal was just the opposite. He taught me to pass through two people and other kinds of passes because it was based on touch. Arvydas Sabonis was probably one of the best big man passers you will ever see. He could thread a needle with the basketball, and it was just so smooth to watch him do it. However, Neal Walk was probably the best in the world that I've ever played with or against.

Regardless of learning to shoot better or to pass the ball, the game is always based on who you're playing against. I played against big Artis Gilmore one time and the jump hook was not going to work against him because he was so strong, and he had so many tricks. He would push you, hold you, pull you out of the air and he wasn't going to run as hard as you thought. There are just so many tricks in basketball. Guys have a very high skill level which makes the game fun and interesting.

Outside of the game, differences between college and professional ball in Europe had to do with how you used your time. We would have two-a-day practices instead of one practice in college. You had to always remember it was a job. We might get up in the morning and have bacon, eggs, a glass of wine and then go to practice. Or we might have bacon, eggs and seltzer water but that was it. They would bring you back after about a two-hour workout and you had lunch around 11:30-12:00. They always had lunch prepared for you. You would have a different pasta and you had a meat. It was weird because every time you had a meal, it was like a three-course meal unless maybe you just stopped somewhere for a slice of pizza. And pizza there is nothing like pizza here in the US. It is so different. After lunch, everybody had siestas; everybody took a nap from about 12:00 to 3:00. Around 3:30 or 4:00 we were back to practice until around 7:00 at night. During those practice sessions, guys were getting shots up or just playing. That was pretty much your day and each day the routine was the same. Occasionally, we might go out to eat dinner, but that was with just the American players. I didn't do that as much because I like to cook. I met this older Italian woman who showed me how to make different pastas and how to cook different things. This also allowed me to save money that would normally go towards eating out all the time.

The Italian league was a summer league and we played all over Italy. We played in Rome, Naples and Bologna. Our season consisted of approximately 30 games. Because our games were in Italy, we didn't have to fly very much. We traveled on these big beautiful buses that were common among teams in the league. Now this was a professional league so if the bus was leaving at a certain time, you had better be there about 30 or 40 minutes before the time to leave. They did not accept players arriving late. If you arrived late, they would leave you and fine you as well. After the league ended, I returned to the US.

It's interesting that I thought I was big and tall until I went to Italy. Many ball players in Europe are tall and big. I laugh now when people say, "Man, you are so big, or you are so tall." I tell them that "You should come and hang out with some of my friends." And many say, "You mean there are people bigger than you." And I say "Yes, by a lot." I was always an outgoing guy, so I met a lot of people in Italy. Today I'm still in touch with a lot of the Italians and guys from Yugoslavia that I met during that time.

JOURNEY TO THE PROMISED LAND

"I've failed over and over and over again in my life.
And that is why I succeed."

Michael Jordan

After my Italian league experience, I returned to the US. I lived in an apartment that my college teammate Walter Daniels had leased. He allowed me to stay in the apartment for a few months. I spent much of that time running and trying to stay in shape for the draft. The hardest thing to do is to stay in shape. To be in tip top shape you must train. You need to train daily and trust me you still would not put in all the work that you need to really stay in shape for basketball. At this point, I still didn't understand that professional basketball was a business. Unfortunately, I didn't really learn that when I was in Italy. I was still just playing ball and having fun. I didn't understand that I had passed the college basketball phase and now this was my profession.

Once you leave college for the pros or even once you leave high school, you must have a different mindset. You must remember that if you're playing then you're taking meals out of someone else's mouth. If you make the team and another player gets cut and doesn't make the team, that affects his wife and kids. But you can't feel bad about the fact that you just took that person's job and their livelihood. You just can't look at it that way. Not at all. And once you understand that it's a business, then you must play the business game of basketball.

In 1980, I was drafted 60th overall in the 3rd round by the San Antonio Spurs. At that time the draft consisted of 10 rounds and 214 players were drafted. Today's draft consists of 2 rounds and 60 picks. In today's draft I would have been a middle of the pack second round pick and probably have received a contract of $700,000 to $1 million dollars per year. Time just wasn't on my business side of the sport. However, it was better for my personal life goals. I went to the Spurs camp after the draft and had a decent camp, but I was cut by the team. A good friend of mine, Ralph Daniels who helped with this book reminded me that back then the league was not as big as it is now. Consequently, the number of jobs were not the same. As a professional player we saw this first-hand because teams had so many guaranteed contracts that it was nearly impossible for players to make teams unless they were the top draft picks. So, guys would make the NBA based on how it was configured back then and not just their talent.

I was talking to a Spurs assistant coach Morris McComb, who was also my junior-year coach at UGA under coach Hugh Durham, and he told me that they were going to send me to Italy again. I didn't want to go back to Italy. I decided to try to make some things happen on my own. I eventually decided to try my luck at a camp with the Atlanta Hawks. The Hawks camp was primarily for their draft picks. I found out quickly that it was mainly a player media presentation for fans and coaching staff. The camp also ended with me being cut. It was at that point that I decided to utilize my talents in another place and that place was Israel.

My journey to Israel was an interesting one and represents a critically important developmental moment both literally and figuratively. I learned later that my introduction to Israel was based on a recommendation from the late Dean Smith, the legendary coach at the University of North Carolina at Chapel Hill. Coach Smith was contacted by Coach Simmy Reguer who was looking for a player for his team in Israel. He needed a player who played the center or power forward position, since a former NBA player decided not to go over to the team; WHY CRY?, a new opportunity. Coach Smith told them that if you want a good center that was being overlooked then go get LaVon Mercer. Coach Smith knew me because he recruited me out of high school. He gave me a glowing recommendation. I also got a recommendation from Leonard Hamilton who is currently the head coach at

Florida State University. Shortly thereafter my agent and I were discussing going to Israel to play.

I vividly remember my first flight to Israel on the now defunct TWA airlines. I thought it was odd that there was no one in the back section of the plane except me. I stretched out across a row of four or five seats and enjoyed the flight. I actually wondered if I was going to the wrong place. And I was still having doubts about leaving the US. Before I left, Coach Hugh Durham offered me a job as an assistant coach for UGA, so that I could complete my degree after I was cut from the Spurs. At the time I was also working part-time at a drugstore. They had already asked me to be a manager in the drugstore. But the opportunity to play in Israel became available and I flew from Atlanta to New York's Kennedy airport and then to Israel.

The empty flight to Israel was a major shock and arriving in Israel was even worse. I had some knowledge of Israel and Jewish culture because of my grandfather and Jewish friends like Bruce Cohen that I met at UGA. I later learned my flight was on the eve of Yom Kippur, the holiest day of the year in Judaism. I landed in Israel and a guy picked me up and he only said, "I need to take you to the hotel." He asked if I had anything to eat and I said, "No, I haven't had anything to eat." He then informed me that it was Yom Kippur. On the way to the hotel we stopped, and he picked up some green grapes and some bottles of water. He took me to the hotel and then disappeared. At this point no one had told me the significance or importance of Yom Kippur. The power was off in the hotel cafeteria and I couldn't get anything to eat. I just had water and green grapes. To this day, I don't really eat those kinds of grapes.

I was in the hotel for the 24 hours during Yom Kippur and the next day the team representative reappeared. The team wanted me to practice early that morning. I hadn't eaten in over a day and I looked like a piece of crap during practice. I still had jet lag and had not eaten any food. I thought they were crazy to ask me to play ball, but that's the business. My first practice was horrible and I'm sure they were thinking I was a terrible player. I suspect they were also thinking they needed to send me back to the US. John Willis, an Israeli American player who became a good friend of mine on Team Hapoel Tel Aviv, talked to me and told me that I wasn't performing. He also verbally stated they were thinking about sending me back to the US, just as I had thought. He said "You gotta pick it up, they may not keep you" or something of that nature. I told him, "This is my first day practicing and I haven't eaten in about two days. I'm just trying to get some food." So, they provided me some food and the next day I looked a little bit better. Interestingly, they didn't tell me the next day we had a game. I had a good lunch and headed off to the game. I knew all the people there were thinking I was not a good player. In the first game I had seven blocked shots, twenty points and fifteen or sixteen rebounds. We won the game and ironically our team had never beaten that team before. Then we played a few more games and we won all the games. They decided they would keep me for a while. The rest became history.

I learned later from players like Darryl Robinson who played with Batar Tel Aviv and helped me recall the Israeli basketball experience for this book, that the threat to send players back was real. They brought him to Israel two months before the season just to watch him practice. They were paying him, but they were mainly bringing him over to evaluate him. Their position about players was we don't know if this guy is going to work out and we may need to send him home. We can always get another American player. The league was an example of the open market at its BEST. If that happens, we need to have some time to get somebody else over here. That was just the European way at the time.

Basketball leagues in Europe are very different than in the states. Today you have a few players who have dual contracts to play in the NBA and their G-league affiliate. Those contracts allow them to play in both leagues. They might play in a G-league game one night and in an NBA game in another city the next night. This practice was common in Europe back then as players played in multiple leagues all the time. In Europe you have the Kurac Cup, and you have the Cup of Cups. And then you had the best team out of each country which made up a league of its own. A team would have had a player that was playing in one of those cups today and the next day he was playing in another cup. This was very confusing for me initially. For example, I might have been in Germany one night and then in Israel the next night. I would have been playing in Haifa one night and then I would come back home and play in Tel Aviv the next night. I always had a bag that was packed and right next to the front door of my home.

Playing in Israel had the added travel issue of dealing with the country's lack of diplomatic ties with other countries. It took me a while to really understand the political aspects of living in Israel. For example, we could not travel from Tel Aviv to Russia which was only a four-hour flight. We would have to fly from Tel Aviv to Switzerland and then from Switzerland to Russia, which would end up being about 10 hours of travel time. We even had to receive special permission to travel there as a team. Things have improved dramatically since that time.

I remember my first European Cup game and it's still one of the most interesting games I have ever played in. We are playing our game in Turkey and the fans were yelling at us and calling us names. It wasn't anything real negative but just fans getting into the game. Every team has what is considered a mascot or flag bearer. Their mascot was a little person and he was running around with the flag on top of this wall. It was totally crazy.

We were in a gym with a concrete wall about five or six feet high surrounding the court. The fans sat behind the wall to watch the game. But in Europe the fans were really into the games and the wall was to prevent them from rushing the court. In Europe fans might come on the court and punch you in the head if they didn't like your performance. Other fans would just throw fifty cent size coins at the opposing team and players. Fans in Greece were especially well known for throwing coins onto the floor. After games you might have to fight your way off the court to get to the locker room. Some of that attitude had to do with their love of their team or maybe a reflection of the high-ticket prices, who knows. The tickets in Europe have always been expensive. Back then a ticket might cost the equivalent of $50 US dollars. Ticket prices were really expensive due to inflation and conversion rates.

We went on to play the game and we won. We then flew back to Israel and everyone on the team was really happy. I believe our coach celebrated a little too much. You must remember that in Europe the teams always send a representative from team management everywhere the team went. Their job was to assess everything that was going on with the team and the game. While we were sitting in the airport preparing to return to Israel, we noticed that the coach was cursing out the team representative. I had no idea what was going on because the coach was speaking Hebrew. I had learned a few

Hebrew words, so I did understand that the coach was calling the team management representative something vulgar. They fired the coach right at the airport. They never gave us a reason why. He was sort of a brash guy and didn't want to be diplomatic as one needed to be in those situations. That same season we went through three or four coaches and team managers.

I probably shouldn't have gone back to that team, but they signed me to a new contract that was twice as much the following season. I thought that was a big improvement, but I learned later that wasn't much at all because they brought me in at the cheapest price. Unfortunately, my agent at the time was focused on other players. He had a reputation among NBA players as a person who you really had to be careful with. I remember discussing this particular agent with Dominique Wilkins who was then starring in the NBA. He had some of the same experiences with agents.

THE EARLY ISRAELI YEARS

"You never know how or when you'll have an impact, or how important your example can be to someone else."

Denzel Washington

Living in Tel Aviv was in some ways very different from living in Atlanta, GA. But in many ways, being in Israel was just like being in the US. People tend to think it's so drastically different, but I would argue that is just not the case. The buildings may be different, but they are still buildings. The people are the same and the routines are the same. You have parks there just like you have here. Tel Aviv has some of the best beaches in the world, and they are a major attraction. You can look 20 yards down into the water and see nothing but clear blue. The whole coast of Israel is absolutely fabulous and a place for Israelis and tourists to enjoy themselves as well as my second home.

Tel Aviv is located on the eastern coast of Israel and borders the Mediterranean Sea. The city is about 40 miles from Jerusalem, less than 500 miles from Cairo, Egypt and about 570 miles from Baghdad, Iraq. I note distances to these cities because most Americans are familiar with the city of Jerusalem and the country of Egypt from the Bible. I also note these cities because of the conflict in the region that most Americans hear about on a daily basis. Understandably, many Americans are also familiar with Baghdad, Iraq from the Persian Gulf wars that began in the early 1990s. Temperatures in Tel Aviv are usually in the 80-90s in the summer and 50-60s in the winter. Tel Aviv was established in 1909 by Yishuv Jews and is the second largest city in Israel after Jerusalem which is the largest. The Tel Aviv architecture resembles much of Europe and consists of many single-story homes. Modern skyscrapers started being built in the late 1960s and construction has kept up with the rest of the world.

Playing basketball in a foreign country can be tough on you, especially in the beginning. You get homesick and you miss your family and friends back home. And you constantly hear all kinds of information, so it's hard to know what is real. But Tel Aviv is a very safe city. However, as you move out of the city and more north near Lebanon, it's probably a bit riskier. The same can be said for areas south of Jerusalem. But overall, living in Tel Aviv was quite similar to living in New York City, Chicago or any other major US city. A great friend of mine Darryl Robinson, who also played in Israel and was from New York City, said he would walk around Tel Aviv alone late at night, yet he would never do that in New York City.

There were other major adjustments that you had to make such as with the food. If you wanted chicken, you couldn't just go to the grocery store and get prepackaged chicken. You had to go to the meat shop or the butcher shop. It was not unusual to receive a chicken with the head still on it and you would have to go home and clean the chicken yourself before you could eat it. And there were no real fast food restaurants back then. You couldn't go to McDonalds for a Big Mac, but you could go to McDavids. McDavids offered hamburgers, but they were very different. So, some of the foods took time to adjust to. You also had to be careful with the water. If you had family or friends coming over to visit, you had to make sure you boiled the water for them because there wasn't too much bottled water at the time.

Getting the news and NBA basketball games was a challenge. I had forgotten about this, but Ralph Daniels who played in Israel in the late 1970s and early 1980s reminded me that in the early 1980's you could only get US magazines like Time, Newsweek and the International Herald Tribune. While he was there playing, USA Today became available. Initially you couldn't see any NBA games and you could only watch one NFL game per week. But at some point, Ralph and other guys would meet up at the Sheraton Hotel on Sunday afternoons to watch a recorded NBA game. There was only one TV station in Israel and similar stations in Jordan and Egypt.

The Jordan TV station mostly focused on the daily actions of the king and queen.

Darryl Robinson and I estimate that the Israeli league was one of the top five leagues in the world excluding the NBA at the time. But just like many large professional sports organizations at that time there could be problems. We knew there were players over there that weren't getting paid or getting paid late. But overall the league was very strong. Other strong and profitable leagues at that time were Italy and Spain. The Israeli league was probably right behind those top tier leagues, unfortunately, most people in America or outside of Europe didn't know that. England and Belgium on the other hand were probably on the lower rung of European leagues. I don't know the rankings of the leagues now but there are currently other countries with competitive leagues like Russia and China that didn't offer contracts to American players.

The first team I played on in Israel was Hapoel Tel Aviv. I played for Hapoel Tel Aviv from 1981-1988. Hapoel Tel Aviv was a good team but management didn't invest money into the team. They were sort of like the New York Knicks of today. They remember their past glory and how good they were, but don't really invest to improve. They also place any failures on everyone except team management.

At the time, the Israeli league was organized around two leagues; the first league and the second league. My team (Hapoel Tel Aviv) was in the first league. You had to win to stay in the first league because each season the bottom two teams in the first league were moved to the second league. In the same way, the top two teams in the second league were moved up to the first league. During my first two years there was a freeze of movement between the two leagues. Then in my third year they changed systems which required you to finish in the top ten to stay in the first league.

As time passed, I started to really learn the complexity of the Israeli league rules. When I signed my first contract with Hapoel Tel Aviv they officially registered me as one of their players. The league rule states that if you are registered as a player with a team then you are part of their team forever. You are supposed to play with them going forward. I learned very quickly that you must know the league rules yourself and you can't rely on agents in the US to understand the rules in European countries. Some agents do not know the rules and others frankly do not care because they are simply trying to get their players signed to a team and get their commission.

After I played for Hapoel Tel Aviv for seven seasons, I learned that technically I couldn't leave the team and stay in Israel playing professional basketball. But I did know that despite the league rules, I had a contract that did in fact give me an option to leave. I also knew it would be difficult to get them to agree to let me leave for another team in Israel.

In the midst of evaluating my satisfaction with the team, I was starting to see that they weren't taking care of players. Frankly they were treating some players very wrong. For example, my teammate, John Willis had an injury that really opened my eyes to the many issues with the team. We were in the gym just shooting around one day before a Kurac Cup game and his back went out. The team decided that they wanted to get rid of him and they didn't want to take care of anything for him. I also started to notice they were bringing in all kinds of guys; some who were not committed to the team. They brought in a guy who spent all his time hanging out and not practicing. When he did practice it was just something stupid. They also brought in a power forward Kenny Labanowski who was a great player, but they wouldn't play him. I just never understood that one. These actions and events had a major impact on me and how I saw the business of basketball now that I had begun to work the business of the game. More importantly, they were a forecast of what was to come with my career in Hapoel Tel Aviv and as a professional athlete.

A NEW COURSE

"You don't make progress by standing on the sidelines, whimpering and complaining. You make progress by implementing ideas."

Shirley Chisolm

After we finished the 1988 season, I decided I was going to leave the Hapoel Tel Aviv team. The Maccabi Tel Aviv team knew that my contract would end soon, and they sent me word they wanted to talk to me. But I couldn't talk to them because I was still under contract with Hapoel Tel Aviv. Because my current contract was ending with Hapoel Tel Aviv, it was time for me to have a meeting with Hapoel Tel Aviv management to talk about my new contract. Hapoel Tel Aviv had a guy who was the manager of the team named Danny Cohen. Cohen said to me "This is the amount of money I'm going to give you. I'm not going to give you any more money so sign the contract and shut up." I was shocked by his attitude and lack of professionalism.

But the real reason I left Hapoel Tel Aviv was he said, *"I own you."* That was, as we say, the nail in the coffin and the exact moment that I knew for sure I would never play for Hapoel Tel Aviv again. That statement immediately and effectively ended my relationship with the Hapoel Tel Aviv team. I was thinking, slavery is over, you don't own me. Cohen was a diehard management type and that's what he really believed. But I decided I was not going to accept that. I was not going to sign the contract or play for Hapoel Tel Aviv ever again.

I don't really know how Maccabi Tel Aviv found out about the contract renegotiation issues, but they approached me. They said as soon as my contract was up, they wanted to talk to me. Interestingly, we played Maccabi Tel Aviv in the championship game my final season with Hapoel Tel Aviv and we lost. Everyone in Israel believed I had already signed a contract with Maccabi Tel Aviv and that was why we lost. That was not true. In fact, I had never even talked to them at that point. Fans need to understand that one person couldn't beat Maccabi Tel Aviv because they had so many great players. They had top flight American and Israeli players. They had Kevin McGee who had been a first round NBA draft pick for the Phoenix Suns and Lee Johnson who was a first-round pick by the Cleveland Cavaliers. They had great players at every position, and they invested money to ensure they had elite talent and a great team every season.

At every stage of the negotiations, Hapoel Tel Aviv continued with the same line; "You're mine and you aren't going anywhere." They told me to just take the money and shut up. I eventually had a meeting with a Maccabi Tel Aviv official named Sham Luke who later became a dear friend of mine. He informed me that Maccabi Tel Aviv wanted to fight the Hapoel Tel Aviv contract and sign me to a contract with their team. We sat down together and went through the Hapoel Tel Aviv contract carefully. It was interesting to me that during the meeting they already had a copy of my Hapoel Tel Aviv contract to share with me and my attorney. My attorney was even more amazed than I was, with Maccabi Tel Aviv's wherewithal to get this done.

During the meeting with my Israeli attorney Leon Goldsmith, Maccabi Tel Aviv told him the same thing they told me. They wanted to fight the contract and sign me with their team. The contract stated that we had to go to arbitration to void the contract. The contract also said I would have to pay Hapoel Tel Aviv compensation to leave. Just before the arbitration hearing, my attorney and I worked out a salary package for me to sign with Maccabi Tel Aviv if I was able to leave Hapoel Tel Aviv.

The day of arbitration, the arbitrator sat up front at a table, Maccabi Tel Aviv and I were at one table and Hapoel Tel Aviv and their people were at another table. Danny Cohen the Hapoel Tel Aviv representative stood up first and started cursing and saying, "He can't go to them, we own him" and so forth. Everyone in the room was stunned to hear him tell another person that he owned them. He continued cursing and saying it over and over because he was so mad about my attempt to leave their team. The Maccabi Tel Aviv representatives then stood up in a far more professional manner to say, "Mr. Mercer has an interest in joining our team and we see in his contract that he can leave. We also understand that we will have to pay some compensation for him to leave." They also indicated that they were willing to work out all the details and understood the need for compensation.

Danny Cohen from Hapoel Tel Aviv then jumped back up and started cursing again and saying, "To hell with him, we own him." The arbitrator then stepped in and said to him, "Sir, sir, you don't own anybody so let's stop that." The arbitrator then called me up to his bench and said, "You understand that we've got a problem here." I said, "Yes, how can we solve it?" He then apologized to me for Danny Cohen's behavior. He said, "He has to understand that nobody owns anybody because of our history, we don't use that word." "But you understand you're going to have to pay some money to leave the team." I said, "Yes, I do understand that and I'm willing to pay compensation because I'm not their slave and I'm not going to play for them again." As I turned to walk back to my table, Cohen starts cursing again and saying, "You Kushi." Kushi means dark skinned person of African descent. But depending upon how you say it, can mean "you Negro." It has very different meanings based on the way you use it. I clearly received the message based on how he said it.

The arbitrator heard all of that from Mr. Cohen and he said to me, "Let's you and I finish this." He then said "Mr. Cohen, we're sorry, but we've told him you don't own him. He does have the right to go to another team and he understands he must compensate you. That's why we're here and I get to tell you how much compensation you will receive." I had already told the arbitrator they weren't paying me a livable wage as an athlete, and they were trying to abuse me. I let him know I wasn't going to stay with Hapoel Tel Aviv even if it meant I had to leave Israel.

The arbitrator took a minute to think and the room sort of went quiet. He then said, "Mr. Mercer you can leave this team. If that's what you want to do, you can. Now this is what you're going to have to pay them." Suddenly came this weird eerie sound. I was thinking it would be somewhere in the neighborhood of $50,000 or $100,000. But the arbitrator said "50 shekels" (I believe) which as the equivalent of around $20. Sham Luke from Maccabi Tel Aviv jumped up, ran over and slammed the money into Danny Cohen's hand. The Hapoel Tel Aviv folks were not saying anything because I believe they were all in shock as much as I was. Sham Luke said to me, "Come on let's go" and we walked out. The Hapoel Tel Aviv fans who were outside the proceedings called me all kinds of vulgar names. I didn't care at that point. I got on a plane and headed back to Atlanta. I had to go back to play against the Hapoel Tel Aviv teams many times thereafter, and we dominated them for the remainder of my career.

I played with the Maccabi Tel Aviv team until my retirement in 1994. Hapoel Tel Aviv loved me when I played for them, but once I changed teams to Maccabi Tel Aviv, I would say they hated me for leaving the organization. On the other hand, I quickly earned the respect and love of the Maccabi Tel Aviv organization and the fans. Maccabi Tel Aviv was very different in that the team had more exposure. We were a great team and we won all the time. I was the first player in Israel to jump from Hapoel Tel Aviv to Maccabi Tel Aviv or just to change teams ever. At that time, you just weren't supposed to leave a team.

Whether Hapoel Tel Aviv or Maccabi Tel Aviv, I experienced many victories and had great times playing in Israel. I was the first Black naturalized player on the Israeli National Team. I played on the 1986 FIBA World Championship team and 1987 EuroBasket championship team. I was on teams that won 6 Israeli Cup Championships (1989, 1990, 1991, 1992, 1994, 1995) and 5 Israeli State Cups (1984, 1989, 1990, 1991, 1994). My Maccabi Tel Aviv teams reached the EuroLeague finals in 1989 and semifinals in 1991. The EuroLeague competition was really strong and many of the stars of that league eventually came to the US to play in the NBA. In the 1989 finals we lost to the Yugoplastika Split team that featured Toni Kukoc and Dino Rada. Kukoc later went on to become a three-time NBA champion with the Chicago Bulls on teams led by Michael Jordan and Scottie Pippen. Rada became a star for the Boston Celtics. Both Kukoc and Rada were voted one of FIBA's 50 greatest players. Rada was also voted a member of the NBA basketball Hall of Fame in 2018.

The move from Hapoel Tel Aviv to Maccabi Tel Aviv is a reminder that professional basketball is not all glamorous. The change in teams impacted friendships and other relationships. Amos Frischman was one of my teammates on the Hapoel Tel Aviv team and his mother and father were my children's (Dionn and Alex) pediatricians. When Dionn was born, his father was the doctor that brought her into the world. When Dionn started requiring medications and check-ups she had to go to his mother; the same thing with Alex. That was the one negative thing about my going from one team to the other was I felt like I hurt people like Amos Frischman in the process. There were many other people who were very mad at me when I left. However, they didn't really know what I was going through so I couldn't focus on that as it was time to move on; WHY CRY?

Looking back there were many aspects of playing professional ball in Israel that were unusual at the time when compared to playing in the US and the NBA. Even in the 1980s and 1990s the teams in Israel never flew without security. Wherever we went there was military personnel on the plane for security. Even if you went to get a glass of water, they wanted to know where you were. Once we were going to play a game in Moscow I believe, and we were coming back through Italy. The day before we arrived in Italy, we were told there was a shooting at the airport and security would be tight. When we arrived, there were these big bullet holes in the walls. Someone had attacked

the Israeli airlines and had killed several people. At that time in the Rome airport, the security wasn't on the ground. Security was on rails that crisscrossed the ceilings. When the shooting broke out, you had shooting from up top and shooting downstairs. One of the terrorists came inside the building and he was killed about 100 yards from where the plane was set to take off. Another guy tried to run around the side where the terrorist came in and he  was killed. Many of the people who were shot were the result of the police shooting to defend the airline passengers from upstairs.

There were also financial implications of playing ball in a foreign country. Most of the guys that played abroad at that time are still trying to figure out the money they made, and the money paid into taxes. In Israel you paid about

51 cents tax on every dollar. The teams would pay the taxes for you, but you had to file the taxes and take care of all the paperwork.

That's one of the things I don't think people really understood. I never really made as much money as people thought, because for seven of my early years I was with a  team unwilling to really compensate its players. That left me with a lot of regret because I was not able to help the people that helped me in the way I wanted to. I especially regret not being able to do more for Momma Sarah and my mother considering how much they had done for me. I just didn't have enough. Many people around me assumed my mother was receiving a lot of money from me, but that was not the case. I paid her rent for a while, but I had to write her a letter to tell her that was coming to an end. Every time I talked to people I was trying to help. Many had the same story............ that they didn't have any money. That was the story of my life with some family and friends when it came to money. They always had more needs than I had money. I did the best with what I had, and I don't feel I had to be the one to provide for everyone. For some, that was enough and for others it was not. I will just have to live with that considering that I learned over time that people will always have a need.

Clockwise: Me as a baby, high schooler and college athlete

Momma Sarah Louise Thomas in her shop in downtown Metter

Herman and Wilfred Thomas

Diane Thomas Oliver

Virginia Thomas Darien and
Michaela Thomas Ellis

Michaela Thomas Ellis serving in Nicaragua

Clockwise: Michaela in Nicaragua, Cee Pee Chavet and holding a machine gun with Willie Sims

Jumping over Kevin McGee and battling with Red Dragon Dino Mengen.

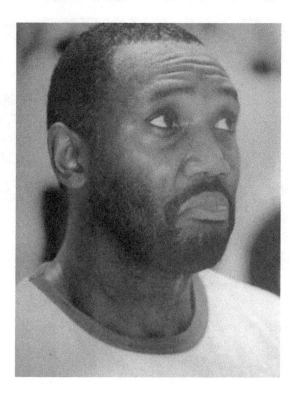

Battling with the guy who opened doors to Israel for me and so many others: Aulcie Perry

Stifling defense

Clockwise: Great pump fake, taking a
break from the action and championship with Doron Jamchi

1975 NBA MVP Bob McAdoo and Earl Cureton

Friends from the beginning: Rick, Reggie, me and Harold

Top to bottom: With old friends Dan Smith, Mike Carter and Kenny Labanowski, me being me and Addie Gordon

Clockwise: Moni Fannon and family, John Willis and Israeli legend Tal Brody and legends of the SEC

Clockwise: NBA Hall of Famers Artis Gilmore, Dominique Wilkins and Dikembe Mutombo

Clockwise: NBA Hall of Famer Dino Rada, Spencer Hayward, Ralph Daniels and Lamar Heard and WNBA stars.

Happy 50th

Working with Palestinian campers in Israel

At Camp Coleman with Bobby Harris

My two young ladies Dionn and Gabby;
both beautiful on the inside and out

Enjoying time with my son Alex

The Lady "My Wife" that cleaned me up and taught me to love again

Supporting Coach West at TEAM FOR CURES 5K Walk/Run

The place where it all began, Metter High School gym

THE ISRAELI BASKETBALL BROTHERS

"Surround yourself only with people who are going to take you higher."

Oprah Winfrey

"You can only be accomplished at something you love."

Maya Angelou

When I arrived in Israel, there were very few Black American players in the Israeli league. If I remember correctly, there were only five other Blacks playing in Israel. It was Aulcie Perry, Earl Williams, Darryl Robinson, Nelson Bailey, Carl Winfrey and me. During the holidays like Thanksgiving and Christmas we would all get together. The most famous Black player at the time was Aulcie Perry who played for the Maccabi Tel Aviv team. Aulcie played college ball at Bethune-Cookman University in Daytona Beach Florida which is less than a four hour's drive from where I grew up in Metter, GA. Aulcie was drafted by the Virginia Squires of the American Basketball Association (ABA) in 1974. After attempts with the Squires, Allentown Jets of the Eastern Professional Basketball League and the New York Knicks he signed with Maccabi Tel Aviv in 1976. The next year Aulcie helped lead Maccabi Tel Aviv to its first EuroLeague championship. I would say Aulcie really opened the door for Black players in Israel and is still a big star in Israel today. Aulcie was more of an Israeli than any of us could ever be. He was a national hero and he dated some of the most beautiful young women in Israel. Aulcie was always invited to all the celebrity events and I would rely on him to get me and Darryl in to those events.

Earl Williams was another Israeli legend that opened the door for me and other players. Earl was a huge physical specimen who probably had shoulders as wide as any NFL football player. He was about 6'8"-6'9" and played college ball at Winston Salem State University. Earl played in the NBA for Phoenix, Detroit Pistons, New York and Boston. In Kareem Abul-Jabbar's book he mentions Earl Williams as one of the best defenders he's ever played against. In 1979 he came to Israel to continue his professional career. Earl was strong as a bull and could really run the floor. He was a great rebounder and had a nice hook shot. The game back then was very physical, and Earl was suited for that kind of play. On most offense plays, he was going to back you down with his physicality. In the early years when I was still playing for Hapoel Tel Aviv, we used to really bang one another in the games. He was one of the pioneers along with Aulcie that really created another opportunity for Black players outside of the US and the NBA. He arrived the year before I started my career with Hapoel Tel Aviv and played on the Maccabi Tel Aviv team that was dominating the league at that time. When Earl was playing, Maccabi Tel Aviv was like the all-star team of the country. If Maccabi Tel Aviv had a game everything shut down in Tel Aviv except for a few restaurants. Everyone seemed to be watching Maccabi Tel Aviv play. Eventually, we earned each other's respect and became really good friends. In those early years we also had to rely on one another for many things. Transportation was one of those things because we all needed a ride for some reason and the only guys who had cars at that time were Aulcie and Earl.

My rookie year I met Darryl Robinson who played for the Batar team. Darryl (or "D" as I call him) recalls that he was sitting eating pizza at a restaurant on Hayarkon street in late August, early September when he saw me a big 6'10" – 7'-footer walking up the street. He knew I was an American and we started talking. Darryl was also a rookie in the Israeli league and had come over after playing at Appalachian State University in Boone NC under Bobby Cremins. Cremins is most known for his time at Georgia Tech and his Atlantic Coast Conference (ACC) teams. But Cremins' first job was at Appalachian State and his first big time recruit was Darryl. Cremins had a long history of recruiting players from New York City and bringing them down south to play ball. Darryl was one of Cremins' first New York City recruits to come south to play. Darryl led Appalachian State to their first NCAA tournament berth under Cremins in 1979. My senior year of high school was Darryl's freshman year at Appalachian State and his team played UGA where I would sign the following year. So, he knew one of my college teammates Walter Daniels. Early in the conversation we knew we had a connection. From that day on we were close friends along with Aulcie Perry and Earl Williams.

Darryl and I quickly become known in Israel in our first year but not to the level of Aulcie and Earl. Because Aulcie and Earl were already household names in Israel, they were already acclimated to the Israeli culture, food and general living. We relied on them to help us with the transition. Darryl and I always got along well. We were good for one another, particularly in this foreign land where support was probably never more important. Our relationship was one that we could challenge each other if we felt the other person was getting off track. We might get pissed off with each other at times, but the relationship allowed us to get over it quickly and move on with life.

Darryl introduced me to fried potatoes and onions for breakfast. And I introduced him to fried chicken for breakfast. We both enjoyed a lot of the same kinds of foods. We were accustomed to having grits flown over to Israel for breakfast and each time Darryl returned from the US he would bring 20 pounds of grits with him as well. He would also have his parents send him pancake mix and syrup around Christmas. In Tel Aviv, we couldn't find the kind of pancake mix we were accustomed to eating in the US. You also couldn't buy Log Cabin or Aunt Jemimah syrup, so we used to have it shipped over to us as well. It's interesting the things you miss when you live abroad. Darryl and I spent a lot of time eating, talking and engaging in a lot of fellowship.

On the court, Darryl was a guy I tried to stay away from. Darryl was one of the smoothest guards I have ever seen. His game was similar to Reggie Theus who played in the NBA in the 1980s. He shot the ball really well and was an excellent ball handler. Darryl saw the game in 3-D, so he was always three steps ahead of everyone else. He knew what was going to happen before anyone else on the floor. I just tried to play off him to try to see what he was seeing.

Nelson Bailey played in Tel Aviv in the same area where Darryl and I played. Nelson was a quiet guy and he was also a great ballplayer. Nelson was a really good scorer and rebounder. He was unique in that he was a power forward-center that could really handle the ball. He would be similar to a Kevin Durant today. When I played him, I always gave him a step and a half because of his quickness. I needed to stop his dribble to have a chance to stop him or block his shot. Carl Winfrey was another guy who played in the Galil which is up near the Lebanon border. If I had to compare Carl to an NBA player today, it would be point guard Chris Paul. He was an excellent ball-handler and scorer but more than anything, he was a great passer.

There were many other really good Black players like Al Flemming, Lee Johnson, Kevin McGee, Willie Sims and Ken Barlow that I either played with or against in the later years of my career. All were just excellent players. The quality of the league improved each year with this influx of talent. The common denominator was all of these brothers could really play. Each had something that they were really good at doing and everything else fell into place for their teams. When we were not playing, we would all get together and hang out. In retrospect, we spent very little time in the gym together because each of us were with our respective teams; practicing and playing or as we would say "on our way to work."

Beyond the Israeli brothers, I learned the game of basketball from players of several generations and in many countries. When I was in high school my favorite player was Dr. J. I used to watch him do stuff that was unbelievable.

The one player that intrigued me the most was George McGinnis because of his strength and shooting ability. McGinnis had a unique one hand pump shot. I couldn't understand how he could control everything with one hand.

At the center position, my favorite players were Kareem Abdul Jabbar and big Bob Lanier. Kareem's skyhook is legendary, and I don't anticipate any player will ever pass him on the NBA all-time scoring list. I really loved Big Bob's ability to take his big feet and move them in any direction to make fabulous moves. If he ever got the ball above his waist it was butter. He could really shoot the ball for a big man. I also liked to see Robert Parrish "The Chief" play the center position. He always looked like "I'm so good, I'm so comfortable. I'm not going to worry about anything." But at the end of the night he would have 25 points and 15 boards. And you never saw him break a sweat. He had the attitude of "I'm just doing this and there is nothing you can do about it." Kareem played the game the same way.

In Israel we had a guy named Mickey Burkowitz. Mickey ran all over the place. He was just a fast-paced player. I played with another guy Doron Jamchi who was just the opposite. Doron could run all day long but Doron never got excited about anything. While Mickey would be yelling and screaming "Let's do it," Doron would be more like "Ok we going to do it." Like a quiet whisper "We are going to win." Mickey and Magic Johnson were similar in that they were rah rah let's get it done and let's win. Doron was more like Larry Bird, would talk trash to you, but when you saw him in the sideline he looked like a quiet little guy. But that quiet dude was an assassin on the court.

There were other guys who played after me that I admired for their intelligence of the game. Shaquille O'Neal is a guy who's most known for his dominance of the game. Yet when I watched him play, I saw his brilliance in the low post. He overpowered most players, but I was always impressed with how he was able to out-think his opposition at the same time. His dominance in the post was more than just his physicality. But let's be real here, his toughness and nastiness in the paint was legendary.

John Stockton was another player who had a very high IQ for the game and was able to dominate even though he was smaller in stature than many of the other players in the league. One of my all-time favorites was Bernard King. He was a highly intelligent player with a lot of fight in him. He was going to keep bringing it to you all game long. He had one of the smoothest and quickest jump shots of all time. He was a guy who was playing to score 100 points against you, but he was happy when he put 30 or 40 on you. Bernard King was a great, great player.

Basketball is not an overly complicated game, but it does require a commitment to learning the game. Learning the game comes from coaching, practicing and observations of other players. Basketball players are the biggest thieves in the world. I say thieves because we copy moves from other players. I've learned a lot from players in the US and from my time playing in Israel and Europe. For example, Neal Walk was a guy I stole from in that I learned how to pass from him. There was a coach in Macon, GA (USA) that we called Duck "Don Richardson" who I stole from because he was the first person to teach me how to shoot a jump hook. So that was something I stole from him. All throughout your career, you find yourself stealing from other players. **I learned early on in my career that by the time you learn to play the game, then you are too old to play the game.** If you are learning the game, then you are constantly evolving as a player.

There is nothing in basketball that is ever the same. You can't go back the next year expecting the season to unfold the same way. Most people have jobs and the job stays pretty much the same year after year. In a business you might have a different client, but the job is still the same. A lawyer will always have his case books that he can look at to pull another person's case to use. But in basketball, it's a consistent growth. All sports in general are constantly changing. That's why the Olympics are so beautiful because you might go out and expect one person to win and the next thing you know, that person isn't even close to winning. On the other hand, the little kid that no one knew anything about is the best thing going. It's all about change and evolving; WHY CRY?

UNUSUAL ACCEPTANCE

"I have a dream that my four children will one day live in a nation where they will not be judged by the color of their skin, but the content of their character."

Martin Luther King Jr.

"I didn't know I was a slave until I found out I couldn't do the things I wanted."

Fredrick Douglass

THERE ARE NO WRONG PEOPLE; THERE ARE WRONG PLACES

One of the many things that was of significant interest to me about Israel was whether I would be accepted or rejected as a Black male. In this world no matter where you go there may be opposition to you because of your race or ethnicity. Intolerance is lurking everywhere. As a Black male, you can walk down the main streets in Atlanta, GA or any city in the US and crazed people may call you out of your name. That's one of those things you must learn to get used to. You must also learn that regardless of what happens in life, you must continue to progress in life.

When I walked down the streets of Tel Aviv, I felt at ease in a different kind of way. It might have been because I was a recognizable professional basketball player. But I don't think it was just that, because I had friends from Kenya and other African nations that lived there who had the same kinds of experiences. When they walked around the city, they received the same types of greetings that I received as a tall Black American basketball player. I have asked others about the issue and none felt that it was simply because I was a recognizable basketball player. Israelis just seemed to offer a different kind of acceptance and experience for everyone living in Israel.

Interestingly, when I would go to Jerusalem, it was the same way. Race was not an issue when you visited the Wailing Wall of Jerusalem. The only real division was the section for males and the section for females. My experiences in Israel were rarely impacted by my race. There just didn't seem to be the same kind of focus on your skin color or pigmentation. I must admit that after experiencing Israel, I became less guarded and eventually more accepting of people regardless of their skin color, race or ethnicity.

In my early years in Israel, I didn't really think about these issues very much. I was just happy to be away from home and had something productive to do. I was happy to have a place to go and to have someone that needed me to do something. Because before arriving in Israel, I just didn't know what I wanted to do. I had been cut by the NBA and I was thinking about staying and working in the US. Israel gave me a new and unexpected opportunity. I was happy to be doing something that I loved and learning a new culture.

But over time, I found myself thinking more about race-related issues and trying to better understand the complexity of the issue. In some ways I began to think about race issues in the same way that I thought about them as I was growing up in the deep South in the US. But I realized I had to think about them from a new perspective. For example, I have deep rooted friendships with many Israelis. Those friendships developed because I found that the State of Israel has love for people regardless of who they are, what they look like or where they come from. Those experiences changed my perspective on many issues. My great friends, Aaron who lives in Gainesville, FL (US) now and Zora Tong who lives in Dallas, TX (US), played a great role in helping me understand the people of Israel.

When I was playing, Tel Aviv was my home. Atlanta was a place to get away and to visit family and friends. Unfortunately, I couldn't get any of my friends or family to come to Israel to visit me because they would say "That's a 12-hour flight and I don't want to go there." When I heard that comment, I would always think, "When was the last time that you were on a plane to go anywhere even if it was a 1-hour flight?" I would also think "What do you really know about Israel other than the few lines you read in a Bible?"

I do want my readers to know that I do understand the complexity of the Israeli-Palestinian issue. When I was in Israel, I had many Israeli and Palestinian friends. I heard the debate and discussion back and forth and from both sides. To me, it seems to go back to Isaac and Ishmael. Two brothers, same father but different mothers. They have been fighting all their lives. If you just leave them alone and let them fight maybe they will knock off each other. But if you ever try to interfere with something one of them is doing, you're going to lose. Same thing with Israel, if you just leave the Israelis alone and let them fight, they may still have a ton of bickering in the community. But they will work out a great deal of their issues. On the contrary, when they have something to fight (like US interference) they will pull together in opposition to the challenge.

There are also many other considerations if you are really trying to understand the issues and actions of Israel. One should ask themselves what you would do if you were constantly under attack? Would you feel bad if you had to drop a bomb on another country that was attacking you? Or would you do whatever was necessary to protect yourself.

In the US we have a lot of comfort because we are so far away from most countries. In some ways the US is very isolated when compared to the many countries in Europe. If someone decided to bomb the US, the missiles would have to travel so far that they would likely be detected. But if you lived in England or France and a European neighbor wanted to drop a missile on you, it could be there in just 20 minutes because of the close proximity. In that case, where would you go? Where would you hide? This contrasts with the US which is so big that if you dropped a bomb in New York, it may not affect anybody in Atlanta or vice versa. On some level, Israelis have to pull together and do the things necessary to take care of themselves.

It reminds me of when I was a kid and I saw the Black community pull together for the greater good of all. If you were in the Black community and you had something, then everybody had something. And the community had the church as the central focus. The religious foundation provided by the church always kept Blacks organized and on some level sort of in line. Today in society the Black community doesn't seem to have the same religious foundation. That seems to be to the detriment of the Black community. At the same time, there is a great focus on prosperity religions. Prosperity religions offer very little to help its members obtain a clear understanding of God. So much of these ministries are all about the "feel good" rather than what we need to know about heaven or the next world. I would ask, how many ministers offer true teaching of God's word? How many address the book of Revelation? How many of them want to talk about: If you don't do this, this is what's going to happen? Or are they simply focused on if you do this then you will receive that in return? It is my belief that this approach does little to improve our understanding of God or His plan for our lives.

In my opinion there is only one God. Now there might be a number of surrogates to reach him, but there's only one God. I personally don't care how you get to God, that's entirely up to you. Some people choose Buddhism, some people choose Christianity, some say they're Muslim, some say they're Jews, some say they're a combination. Then there are others who say what difference does it make. The question is do you have the spiritual foundation to deal with God?

Understanding the people in the State of Israel can offer a lot to our general understanding of what different groups of people have gone through over the years. Most understand the plight of African Americans and having to fight through slavery in the US. We also know that there were a lot of slaves in Africa. Some African Americans served as indentured slaves for people in Africa before arriving in America. Some were forced to get on a ship and come to America just to be another type of slave.

The bigger message is that all throughout history, there have always been groups of people who have tried to hold others down. I'm saddened that the average Israeli my age has known war and hostility their entire life. Their daily lives are impacted by their religion and faith which is less common in the US; race is more likely to impact people in the US.

Many Israelis argue "we've been slaves too" as the Jews have been enslaved across time. Interestingly, many don't realize there are Blacks in Israel who are Jewish or have the Jewish heritage that are not accepted even though they grew up in that same region. There are also some Ethiopians who are not accepted in the region. One must also consider that some Ethiopians don't accept African Americans. In fact, there are a lot of Africans who believe the oppression of African Americans is our fault for staying in the US after slavery ended. So, when you start looking at a term like racism, you must evaluate it in the totality of all individuals regardless of what they look like. Some are quick to apply it only to White males or White individuals in general. But there are instances of racism among individuals who look similar. The diversity that is in Israel has added a lot to my thought process about race. Those observations have forced me to look beyond the traditional and singular narrative when it comes to how race plays into acceptance.

Intertwined in the traditional concept of racism is the issue of classism which is getting significant attention in the US. Or any type of "ism" where one group is perceived better or of a higher status than another. Even in southeast GA when I was a kid there were people of different classes regardless of what race they were from. You had Blacks that were in one position and other Blacks that were in a perceived lower position.

Consequently, you had one Black group that was looking at or up to another Black group in ways that were not healthy for the community overall.

Some of these same class issues appear to exist today in settings that I did not anticipate. I have worked on and with some of the most well-known historically Black institutions of higher education in the USA. One thing that drove me absolutely crazy was to see the distinction between someone Black with a PhD versus someone White with a PhD in a battle of class-ism. In my humble view some of the Black PhD professors didn't seem to operate as an equal participant to the White PhD professors. Sometimes their actions suggested they did not feel equal to the White, Indian or the Asian PhD professors. In some ways they seemed to be operating on a lower level than their counterparts instead of thinking "I am absolutely equal to my colleagues." In stating that, my feeling is everyone else in our community will take guidance from their hubris that we can succeed as they "Black PhD professors" have done. They are truly the communities' future by their show of pride!

I'm sure this is a complicated issue that I don't completely understand but it was very noticeable. But my brother-n-law who's in academia reminds me that academia is a very complex work environment that exposes many issues related to individual people. Although there are colleges and departments within universities, ultimately confidence and subsequently success in that environment is based on individual performance rather than the greater college or department performance. At the same time, individual performance and success can be impacted by internal and external factors such as bias, race, seniority, the training obtained during the PhD process, post PhD mentor-ship and career guidance. Differences in these internal and external factors result in different confidence and self-worth levels in that setting that may have translated into my observations. And he notes that the culture of institutions is highly variable which also deferentially impacts academicians.

But ultimately, he says it boils down to how the individual responds in their academic setting. Despite the challenges, the confident and successful academician whether White, Black, Green or Brown will stay focused on the tasks at hand while striving to develop and maintain a unique identity separate from their role in academia. Because in the end, it's just a job to keep the bills paid and to hopefully make a difference. If the job, whether in academia or otherwise becomes one's life, they have an even bigger problem that has little to do with the job itself.

The major lessons that I've learned about acceptance as a result of living in the US and Israel is that true acceptance can be hard to capture. Maybe some perceived acceptance is the result of a special talent or what you are bringing to the table or relationship. The other influential aspect may be related to whether the perspective is from the person seeking acceptance or the person making the determination about acceptance. Additionally, one must consider how internal experiences and biases factor into acceptance or lack of acceptance.

In some respects, the world appears to be moving to greater acceptance of some groups and less of others. It is possible that the greater perceptions of acceptance are not acceptance at all but simply tolerance. I am not sure how we should reconcile these differences or how to break down the barriers that contribute to inequality. I will likely spend the rest of my life thinking about these issues while also trying to figure out ways to contribute positively.

CONVERSION

"This is my simple religion. There is no need for temples; no need for complicated philosophy. Our own brain, our own heart is our temple; the philosophy is kindness."

Dalai Lama

LAVON BEN ABRAHAM

My conversion to Judaism is not something I will expect most people to understand and for others to accept. But at this stage in life I choose not to devote a lot of energy to issues about my life that people disagree with and that do not affect them. In my heart it was the right decision. Many American Jews simply say there are no Black Jews. Others do not believe in the conversion process; either one is born a Jew, or they are not. I did not take the decision of conversion lightly and once the process started, I knew it was the right one and there was no turning back. The process is not complex but requires a firm lifelong commitment to learning and understanding Judaism and of course living a disciplined and righteous life. People who decide to convert can experience significant backlash from their own families and communities and some pushback from the greater Jewish community. Coming to the decision of conversion should not be taken lightly as it will test your innermost being and translate into a new identity in God.

It's interesting that growing up in South GA and in the Bible belt in general, I knew very little other than being a Baptist. In my world there were Methodist, Baptists and maybe in larger cities like Savannah you might find some Catholics. I don't recall seeing a Church of God or Church of God in Christ or Church of Christ back then. In the Black community it was all about going to a Baptist church. You had your Whatever Whatever Baptist Church or your Whatever Whatever Street Baptist Church and you had your Primitive Baptist Church, First Baptist Church and the Missionary Baptist Churches. Regardless of the name, the Baptist church was the foundation of the community for Black people of that day.

Even though I was the grandson of a Baptist minister, I don't recall really studying the Bible in great detail to understand its meaning. I knew there was an Old Testament and a New Testament. I could of course recite some of the stories of the Bible and I knew many of the books of the Bible. So, the required study during the conversion process was both stimulating and enlightening to me. The process requires a few basics which include: comprehensive and "mentored" study, circumcision if you are not already circumcised, an evaluation of readiness, immersion in a ritual pool (mikveh) and the acceptance of a Hebrew name.

The conversion to Judaism started with my interest in staying in Israel permanently. If you get a chance to go to Israel, you will quickly see that there is no major difference between being in Israel or in the US. It does get a little hotter, which is saying something after growing up in the southern part of Georgia. The people in Israel are lovely people. The language is different but there are many individuals who speak English. On the other hand, the language barrier creates an opportunity for new learning. I did attend some classes to learn Hebrew, but I wouldn't say that I'm an expert or even fluent speaker. My coaches spoke both English and Hebrew and we frequently had translators on the team to help us understand the intricacies of the game that you can't see when you're on the floor.

I was interested in Israeli citizenship and dual citizenship with the US. There are only a few countries that you can have dual citizenship with the US. Israel is one of those countries. I knew that all Israeli citizens must serve in the Israeli Defense Force (IDF). An immediate question that I received during the process of evaluating dual citizenship was "Are you going to become Jewish?" Receiving citizenship in Israel is not tied to conversion to Judaism but it was a question I was asked frequently as I was seeking out the steps for permanent citizenship. I understood that I would probably need to consider my religious beliefs and how those would or would not align with the beliefs of my friends and many others in the region. In considering the conversion, I realized my grandfather was a Baptist minister and we practiced Old and New Testament. After some thoughtful consideration I decided I was staying in Israel and conversion would allow full immersion and commitment. It wasn't simply that I needed to change to Judaism because I was interacting with mostly Jews in Israel. It was part of a broader search for the truth and an examination of who I was as a person. One must remember, at this stage in my life I wasn't planning to return to the US. I was planning to continue my life in Israel. At the time, I was married and I decided this was the right decision for me and my family.

In the first phase when comprehensive study under the direction of a Rabbi occurs, I did not complete my study in Israel. I received my instruction and counsel under the tutelage of a Rabbi in Miami, FL. I met the Rabbi there and told him what I was thinking of doing and his first question was "Are you sure that's what you want to do?" He gave me a lot of literature and I started studying the extensive information that he provided. Over the next year I took classes to improve my understanding and knowledge. When I returned to Israel the next summer, the conversion was complete. I did get a lot of help from people in Israel, but my primary mentorship was under the Rabbi in Miami. That worked better as the mentorship had to occur in English because I could not read Hebrew. There was a comprehensive test at the end of the mentoring process to ensure that I had a full understanding of Judaism. At the end of the process, the Hebrew name given was LaVon Ben Abraham or LaVon son of Abraham. And as you would expect there was paperwork that I had to complete that was sent to the US Embassy in Tel Aviv.

There is a post-conversion period which can be very challenging for some as relationships with some friends and families may become strained or awkward as they try to process your major life change. The key here is "it's your life." I don't think I experienced much resistance to the conversion, but I did receive frequent comments that suggested the Israeli's might be brainwashing me. I am a strong-minded individual and comments that are filled with inadequate information have little impact on my day-to-day sense of being.

Today I would say I practice Old and New Testament. Some might say that I am a Messianic Jew as I practice aspects of Judaism and Christianity. Messianic Jews believe that Jesus is the Messiah and died for the sins of the world. They also believe that the Jews are the chosen people and they must obey the laws of the Torah and observe Jewish holidays. Regardless of what I am considered by others, I consider myself an individual trying to live a righteous life in the eyes of God and humanity.

A CALL TO SERVE

"Not everything that is faced can be changed; but nothing can be changed until it is faced."

James Baldwin

FAITH IS BOTH BELIEF AND BEHAVIOR

I've learned over the years that someone who has been blessed with as much as I have, must give something back. I believe everything in life is really connected to service. Four people that lived long and peaceful lives and gave substantial service were my dad Curly Byrd, Boss Lowery, Coach West and Momma Sarah. They were always giving back to somebody else. They worked hard and they were always willing to help others. To them, it was always about service. They all might say, "LaVon we are going to do this, but we gotta go help this person first."

Coach West was our basketball coach, but he was also a guy who served us by thinking beyond basketball to understanding our individual needs. So, he would work with me on an individual level and discuss things with me as a young man separate from the team. He did the exact same with other players. For example, he would have personal conversations with Herman just about academics. He knew Herman was a really smart kid and he needed to make sure he kept his eyes on his grades.

Coach also had private conversations with Bruce Collins. Bruce was one of the few of us who had a father in the home and who was an educator. Bruce was headed down another positive trajectory because of that support. Coach had many team conversations with us, but his greatest strength was his ability to connect with us individually. He was a servant leader at that time even though we probably had no idea what that meant. I would say the same thing for Momma Sarah. She would tell me some things she wouldn't tell Herman because she felt I needed to know the information more than he needed to know it. She always seemed to have information that we all needed to know but not necessarily as a group.

I served in the Israeli military because I wanted to stay in Israel. I wanted to give something back and had to serve based on citizenship. Actually, I didn't think I was coming back to the US after I retired from playing basketball. I really loved living in Israel. I have visited many countries throughout Europe and Israel remains at the top. In the military I was able to blend in and do what I was supposed to do. I met a lot of different friends in the military that were totally different from the basketball world. When I went into the Army, I was in this group of guys some of them who had converted to Judaism and were coming over to stay in Israel. I'm not  talking about just basketball guys, but people in general. They were doing Aliyah or moving back to their homeland. But even when you move back, you still must do your military service. So, I was doing my military service to become a citizen.

Serving in the military was a rude awakening to the world outside of basketball. When you enter the army, they measure you and they give you shoes. Because of my foot size, I didn't have boots for the first two weeks. I had to run around in tennis shoes. Because of my height, they didn't have a uniform for me either. To create one, they took two pair of pants and stitched them together so that I would have pants. They created three pairs of pants in that manner. They did the same thing with shirts by stitching two sleeves together so that it would fit me.

In the beginning of my service I went to this place called Bata Arbba that no longer exists. Bata Arbba was part of the land Israelis gave back to the Palestinians up above Jerusalem. I would train in the morning which consisted of a lot of running. They put us in barracks, and I took the bottom bunk near the door. My bunkmate was an Arab Israeli fighting with the Israelis. He spoke Arabic and Hebrew but couldn't speak any English. I spoke a little Hebrew and English and we become friends despite the initial communication barrier.

One night we were on patrol and our job was to protect the barracks where we were living. We were out walking around, and we didn't expect any activity. But all of a sudden, we heard "tick tick," "tick tick" and we both thought "What the?" He looked at me and I looked at him totally surprised. So, we started walking around the building. I went one way and he went the other. Imagine this, I'm 6'10" with an M-16 that has a loaded magazine in it. I didn't care who it was, I was going to shoot them because this was a dangerous area. When we came around the building, we saw a guy who was from New York trying to kill himself. He was so stressed out because he could not deal with being in Israel. He was losing his mind and trying to kill himself. So, we took his gun. There is a pin in an M-16 about ¾ inch long and if you remove that pin, then the gun would not work. You couldn't shoot it or do anything else other than maybe hit someone over the head with it. We took the pin from the gun and took the magazine out of the gun. We gave the gun back to him and then we made him go back inside. Later that night we were relieved after our shift and the commander came to talk to us. We told him what happened, and he said "WHAT!" He was totally shocked. Early the next morning we went outside, and there was a car to pick the soldier up. They took him directly to the mental hospital in Jerusalem. They didn't want to take any chances with him.

Because we did such a good job, they put us in front of the entire headquarters and barracks where everyone lived. To the right of our location was a settlement where some religious Jews were staying to occupy the land.

The road leading up to our location was about 75 yards. The commander gave us specific instructions to stop any car coming up too fast on this road. He specifically said, "I don't care what you do, I want you to stop any car and get them to slow down." He instructed us to raise our gun and if the car did not slow down then shoot the individual driving the car. One night we saw a car approaching us too fast. We aimed our guns and we were about to fire when all of a sudden, the guy slammed on his breaks. We went to the car and the guy said, "I'm sorry, I'm sorry, I'm sorry." We allowed him to proceed to the settlement, but this made us very nervous. It was very dangerous out there and you had to protect yourself everywhere you went.

After I entered the reserves, my main role for the Israeli government was to make sure that I supported the kids of fathers killed in the military. I was involved in a wide range of sporting events. That's when I started to understand what was happening. I was involved with the kids during basketball and soccer events. We would complete our reserve duties and organize camps for the kids to teach them about sports. We became like surrogate brothers to these kids. I was able to meet a lot of wonderful kids in that role. Those experiences translated over to me completing speaking engagements about Israeli culture once I returned to the US. It's a part of my goal of giving back to the State of Israel that has given so much to me.

Technically, I would have stayed in the Israeli Army until the age of 55. If I had gone back to Israel at age 50, I would have still been in the reserves. A lot of kids are trying to fight being in the military now. Mandatory service made the country stronger because everyone was committed. You must give a part of your life to your country to be a citizen there. If everybody had to serve in the US, it would make a difference and the moral compass would be different.

Interestingly, by serving in the Israeli military I knew more about what was going on in the US than most US citizens. Because we like most military organizations had intel on other countries. There were things going on in the US that Americans didn't even know about. During my first year in Israel, I was sitting in my apartment watching Anwar Sadat when all of a sudden, I saw his assassination. I was thinking my God what have I gotten myself into?

I have been fortunate to continue my service to society after returning to the US in ways that align with both basketball and my experiences in Israel. For the past 20 years I have been able to serve at camps organized by my long-time friend Bobby Harris. Bobby is a Jewish-American who says he's known me since I was a junior in high school. He first saw me at one of the Dapper Dan Roundball Classic tournaments in Pittsburgh, PA. The Dapper Dan tournaments were designed to bring in the best high school basketball prospects to compete against one another. I didn't meet him at the camp but in 1981 he saw me again in Israel when I was a member of an Israeli all-star team playing a game against NBA all-stars. After my retirement and return to the US, he saw an article about me returning to Atlanta in the Jewish Times newspaper. He called me and invited me to one of his camps called "Camp Coleman." We have been great friends since that initial camp.

The camps are very therapeutic for me as they allow me to spend time mentoring kids and talking about my experiences in Israel. My discussions are not just about being a ball player, but also as a naturalized citizen of the State of Israel. The kids are at an age where they are truly open to mentoring and eager to learn about Israel beyond the misrepresentation that frequently occurs on TV. It's an opportunity for me to explain my core principles that center around honesty, integrity, fairness and truth. It's also a time to break down the walls of race and religion and focus on our unique differences and what can be learned from our collective experiences. At each visit, it is my hope that I can inform, educate, uplift and encourage while facilitating unity and reducing the focus on negative differences. Bobby continues to invite me back year after year so I must assume that something positive is emerging from those experiences.

I must share a story that highlights the purity of kids and the unexpected benefits of engaging in mentoring activities. On a visit to one of Bobby's camps and just a few weeks after the passing of my  good friend and NBA great Darryl Dawkins, a beautiful young girl came up to me in tears and said, "I thought you died." Darryl had been a previous camp mentor. The news of his death had been discussed before my arrival at one of the camps. It's just a reminder that kids are more concerned and insightful than we often give them credit. To her in that moment Darryl and I were simply two African American 7-foot basketball players one of which had died. His death certainly touched her. I am thankful for these mentoring opportunities and certainly thankful for my friendship with my late friend Darryl Dawkins.

Another great guy who has given me a similar opportunity to continue to serve in the Atlanta area is Gary Sobel. Gary is a leader of an organization designed to support the soldiers of the IDF called Friends of the IDF or FIDF. We have been able to get to know each other through this organization over the last decade. FIDF allows me an opportunity to speak and offer some thoughts about Israel and life in general. I don't have an official role and that doesn't matter. Service activities make me feel that I'm contributing to society in some meaningful way and making a difference. One unanticipated benefit of service activities is what you learn from and about people and what you learn from them about yourself. In his interview, Gary noted that he has never seen me play basketball and he doesn't really see me as a basketball player. He indicated there may not be one word to describe me but when he thinks of me, he smiles. That is a very high compliment and one that I am very appreciative to receive.

It is important for me to let people know that I first learned service from my dad, family members, Buddy Mason (who was a mentor at UGA) and Momma Sarah. There are no words to adequately acknowledge how their service to me impacted my life. During my time with Momma Sarah she worked to meet our needs regardless of whether it was in her best interest.

Three of Momma Sarah's children, Herman, Wilfred, and Diane, all served in the US Army. Similarly, my biological brothers Jeffrey and Randy served in the US Navy. I note their military service because the US military goes great lengths to protect this country and the freedoms that we all have. I'm not sure who said it first but the saying that "freedom ain't free" is real. I have seen examples of this both in the US and Israel. Herman and Wilfred both had long and decorated military careers and I am very proud of them. So, while I was pursuing my dream of professional basketball, my brothers and sisters were in the US doing the real work that has offered me the freedom to travel abroad and achieve those dreams.

Michelle who was just a little girl and our pregame hair stylist when I lived with them also has a commitment to serving others in Central America. She is part of a team of Christians led by Lowell and Angie Hoover of Charleston, SC who have dedicated themselves to improving the lives of people who operate in extreme poverty and at times civil unrest. Their mission team has worked tirelessly to improve access to medical care in Malpaisillo, a small poverty-stricken community in central Nicaragua. As part of those efforts, their church (Charleston Church of Christ) raised the necessary funds to build a small medical clinic that offers free medical care to the local community. Like so many of my family members, Michelle identified an opportunity to serve and dedicated herself to improving the lives of someone other than just herself.

But these Thomas and Byrd family efforts are the traditional outward service activities. They have extended themselves in ways that people who claim to know them do not know. Diane who recently lost her only son is the guardian of his son, her grandson. Even in tragedy she continues to serve. Some will read this and say well that's what you should do. And that is true but clearly that is not happening consistently in America. Many families allow their loved ones to enter into the foster care system because they don't want to step in and be bothered by children that are not their own. So, if that is what everyone should be doing, then why is the foster care system so overloaded with children?

In addition to her missionary work, Michelle is an adoptive mom. Few people know that. In the same way, Wilfred is what I would consider a surrogate father to a child of a female soldier who was in his Army unit years ago. It is possible that Momma Sarah passed down those characteristics to them genetically. I don't know. In my case, she passed it down to me in action and spirit. I suspect that we all learned it from just listening and watching humble service in action rather than a bunch of pointless talk. So, service to society among other things is why I'm proud to call the Thomas family, my family. They represent the kind of service-oriented attitudes, goodness and love that is less common today but so desperately needed. Their actions force me to ask each day, "What have you given back today?"

WHAT THEY DON'T KNOW

"To know how much there is to know is the beginning of learning to live."

Dorothy West

It's always interesting to hear the American perspective of Israel. I am not a historian or an expert of everything Israel. But I lived there 15 years and have had the experience of seeing things from the inside. That lived experienced gives me some insights into the cultural, political and social dynamics that exist in Israel and how they differ from beliefs and perspectives of the US. When I was there Israelis showed a lot of love to Americans. There were many times that we went out and didn't pay for anything. I don't think it was just because we were ball players. Some said they loved the way Americans lived. The American players on the bigger teams were especially loved dearly.

I believe many Americans naturally think they wouldn't go to Israel because there is so much war. They see the news about issues in the West Bank and Gaza Strip and that is scary. But the US news frequently does not communicate the total context. There are certainly times that Israel is dangerous just as there is danger in the Southside of Chicago or areas in New York City. But to outsiders, it seems to be more than just war. It is important for my American friends to understand that Israel is in a constant state of alert. For them it's all about defense rather than initiating wars. The US news frequently shows the military side of Israel or Israel defending itself which is interpreted as aggressive behavior. But much of what is perceived about Israel does not capture the fact that everything is about its survival. Israel does want peace despite what the outside world thinks.

Many Americans and particularly those with any sort of religious background see Israel as simply the land where Jesus walked and of course Israel is the "promised land." It does not consider the longstanding conflict between the Israelis and Palestinians or the impact of different political regimes or actions of people on both sides of the conflict. I also find many Americans cannot see Jesus as a Jew....... but only as a Christian. There is an interesting book "What Every Christian Needs to Know About the Jewishness of Jesus" by Rabbi Evan Moffic which gets into the issue. Jesus was not a Christian, he was a Jew that lived, breathed and died a Jew. The book explains in detail how many of Jesus' teachings were based on his Jewish upbringing, Jewish faith and Jewish culture at the time. Similarly, the outcome of his ministry was Christianity that so many follow today. **[But more importantly, it makes the point that Jews and Christians need to talk to one another more to gain a better understanding of the different perspectives and many similarities.]**

Communication ultimately improves clarity and understanding. Jesus' followers were "later" called Christians "followers of Christ" first in the book of Acts, Chapter 11. Luke wrote "and the disciples were called Christians first in Antioch." It's a simple reminder of the interrelationship between Judaism and Christianity. So, to me any evaluations or opinions about Israel must consider the history and culture of the time and in the context of the complex political changes over time. Opinions about Israel would be better supported by a visit there to really understand the total context.

It is not my attempt to make any religious or political argument regarding the merits or negativities of Israel or the Jewish or Christian faiths. My goal is to encourage the many who have such strong opinions about Israel and the different faiths that exist worldwide, to do their homework. I encourage them to explore the long and complicated histories of Israel, Judaism as well as other faiths. I would also say take a trip to Israel because most people who offer thoughts about Israel have never been there. For most (including myself), our knowledge and understanding is incomplete, therefore our strong opinions maybe lacking the necessary information to have such opinions. To my US family and friends, I would also recommend reading "Misreading Scripture With Western Eyes: Removing Cultural Blinders to

Better Understand the Bible" by E. Randolph Richards and Brandon J. O'Brien. This book offers great insights into this issue and serves as a reminder that the Bible was not written in the context of Western culture. The contents of the Bible are oftentimes not entirely clear to us today. The book also highlights the differences between the culture at the time the Bible was written and our modern and Western view. Finally, the book demonstrates how these collective differences impact how we interpret and understand scripture.

In addition to the complex issues related to religion in Israel, it is important for me to reiterate the role that race or skin color played in my experiences. Being a Black person in Israel was a rarity. If you rode the bus you might notice people staring at you. Some would even want to touch your skin which was quite weird. Now being an almost seven-foot-tall Black guy brought its own intrigue. There were some however, who had the same kinds of issues with Blacks as some Americans do. They would use the word "Kushi" in the same way the word n----- is still used today. Darryl and I both experienced the negative side of that word while in Israel. It didn't bother most of us in the beginning but over time it did. Some in Israel would say we don't have racial problems which may have been true relative to the religious issues between Jews and Arabs. There are Arabs who are Israeli citizens and that speak fluent Hebrew but are considered what is the equivalent of second-class citizens. That made me uncomfortable as that was the same kind of treatment Blacks living in the southern US experienced during my formative years and today has a chokehold on America.

The State of Israel is just as much a cultural melting pot as major US cities like New York that have long histories of immigrants coming to the US. My experiences there differ from the beliefs most Americans have about Israel which center around war and religion. Even today Israel is a very safe country and the annual number of murders is relatively low and somewhere around 2.4 per 100,000 residents for a country that has a population of 8.6 million residents. I suspect rates were even lower when I lived there. In 2016 the murder rate in the largest city in the US, New York City, was 3.4 per 100,000. Chicago which has 2.7 million residents has a murder rate of 10.2 per 100,000. This is just one statistic for comparison. Israel is far more than just bombs which is usually the first thing I hear when the topic of Israel emerges. It was not unusual for me and other players to be out by ourselves at 3 or 4 in the morning walking alone without any fear. I'm not sure if I would do that in New York or Chicago today. Many Americans think it's just a place of war and hostility and a third world country. It's far from that. Also, many of the security measures in the US that started after 9-11 were in place in Israel in the 1980s. Having to take off your shoes at the airport and other extra security measures were standard practice when I played in Israel in the 1980s and 1990s.

In his interview for this book, my good friend Darryl reminded me of the unique groups of American born citizens living in Israel that few Americans know about. About 50 years ago a group of Black Americans who call themselves the Black Israelites, started leaving major cities like New York, Philadelphia, Los Angeles and Newark to escape the racism of the US. Many live in the city of Dimona which is due south of Jerusalem and about 22 miles south of Be'er Sheva and 22 miles west of the Dead Sea. Many Black American players were told by Israelis to be careful with them because they were radicals. We were of course even more curious and interested to hear their stories. So, we talked to them about their experiences. Maybe we simply talked to them because they were Black people living in Israel which was uncommon. We found them to be really good people. They had their own successful schools and jobs in their communities which was quite different from what we had seen in the US.

I would also say that most non-Jewish Americans that talk to me about Israel are surprised to know that Israel is not a very religious country. And there is not just one religion there. Interestingly, one could also find a Baptist village in Israel which helps Christians with their beliefs and their spiritual journey. Others would also be surprised to know that Israel is also a very liberal country. I would say that there are regions in the US such as the southern Bible belt that are far more religious and conservative. These US regions are also more likely to espouse ideology that is aligned with racism and separatism. I would say only about 10% of Israelis citizens are orthodox Jews.

I had very positive experiences with Arabs and Jews in Israel regardless of their background. I broke bread with both Arabs and Jews in their homes. It was much harder to tell Jews from Arabs in Israel than most people think. There are signs such as clothing, hats and hair styles, but skin color which can be such a focus in the US cannot be solely used to distinguish them. In general, most Arabs are darker skinned people who looked like African Americans; but some do have lighter skin. Many people outside of Israel don't realize there are Israeli Jews that also have dark skin so you can be fooled. The lesson learned was don't focus to much on skin color.

The main thing that people do not know or understand is that the correct perspective can only be achieved by seeing things from all sides. Steve Jobs, the co-founder of Apple said *"A lot of people in our industry haven't had very diverse experiences. So, they don't have enough dots to connect, and they end up with very linear solutions without a broad perspective on the problem. The broader one's understanding of the human experience, the better design we will have.*" Now clearly, he was thinking about the computer or tech industry, but these thoughts offer great insights into how a limited view of things in general can negatively impact one's understanding and experiences. I hear a lot of criticism about Israel from people who have never been to Israel. In the same way there is criticism of the US from people who have never visited the US.

Television and particularly the news can quickly distort one's view of things and create misperceptions about countries or people that are short sighted and inaccurate. I'm not saying that I have the only correct perspective because that would be foolish and not true. But I would say that having traveled to many countries around the world has offered me insights into issues because of having a broader perspective. That perspective has been created by interacting with people from many countries and cultures.

A lot of my perspective began with seeing Momma Sarah taking a chance on me and having a bigger vision for me than I had for myself. I think she instilled that in all of us and consequently we sought out different things than many of our contemporaries. Diane, Herman and Wilfred traveled extensively in the military and have seen a lot of things. A short conversation with them can be very enlightening as you begin to hear about what they have seen and the places where they have been; at least the ones they can tell you about. My brother Jeffery was the only one to come to Israel to see me and it was an enlightening experience. The two of us were able to spend time halfway around the world. It was very amazing that two small town guys were able to kick the lights out in Tel Aviv.

In the same way, Michelle has traveled to Europe and Central America and consequently she has a unique perspective on things like poverty and access to care. Her heart for people comes from Momma Sarah of course but was enhanced by her travel and seeing things that most people have not seen. Until one has seen how others around the world live and operate, it is hard to really understand the complexity of issues that plague this world. I would challenge anyone who has a negative thought about Israel or any country for that matter, to actually go there before offering their next strong opinion. Go there and see this beautiful country that is controversial, complex and oftentimes misunderstood. Don't rely on a narrow perspective created by misinterpretations of the Bible or modern-day news stories.

WHAT YOU GO THROUGH TO GET TO

"Never underestimate the power of dreams and the influence of the human spirit. We are all the same in notion: The potential for greatness lives with each of us."

Wilma Rudolph

Adversity is a word that a lot of people use who come from backgrounds like mine. In my view, the word adversity has no real meaning. Challenge is probably the word I would use. I realize it probably means the same thing as adversity, but I view my life as more of a challenge than the traditional sense of adversity. I learned a long time ago that life is a series of challenges and through those challenges (and at times failure) there is a lesson. And with each lesson one must take the outcome and move forward. There will always be someone who is ready to tell you what you can't do or that you won't be successful. But that is simply their opinion. I've had so many people in my life tell me what I couldn't do. It's very sad that I haven't had as many of them tell me what I could do. Had I listened to those naysayers I wouldn't be where I am today, and you wouldn't be reading this book.

I am proud to have come from a small town. A lot of people who come from Metter and other small towns started their lives in challenging situations. Many of them just decided to work hard to improve their lives regardless of their situation. Many grew up with very little and had to play ball in sandlots or poorly maintained courts. Those same individuals have accomplished just as much in life as people from the city who came from more affluent homes.

Sometimes society creates unnecessary challenges. Society can create unnecessary challenge by the harshness that it offers kids or the poor self confidence that it facilitates in them. Some in society might say "He ain't nothing or he's stupid" or "He's not going to do this or he's not going to do that" just because of their poverty filled backgrounds. And society at times focuses on just the affluent kids who can afford private schools or locations where they are predestined to be great. They receive more positivity and encouragement in the form of "He's going to do this and he's going to be the best and he's going to do all this stuff." Little attention has been given to the impact that these negative beliefs/attitudes about an individual can have on their self-esteem and ultimately how it influences their actions and progress in life. Consequently, most people don't give much thought to or understand the "going through part."

It's interesting to think about the things that were commonplace in my early life in Metter that created unnecessary challenges. Despite them being in our daily lives we gave very little thought to them at the time as we understood they were just the things we had to go through. Today these same events seem almost impossible. I lived in the remnants of the segregated South and slavery, racial tensions and undercurrent were always present. But can you imagine living in any place in the US in the 1980s that allowed the Klu Klux Klan to receive permits from the city to march in the city's annual spring parade. Each year the town of Metter holds the Blooming Festival in the Spring on Easter weekend. It was common even in the 1980s to see the KKK march during those parades. The rationale for that kind of decision was quite confusing but that was just how it was.

Even until 1999 or 2000 the high school continued to hold separate proms based on race. The general explanation was the cost of using the country club was higher than Black families were willing to pay. So, the White kids had a prom at the country club and the Black kids held their prom at the local community center. I have been asked many times, "How did that work?" Well for class meetings an announcement would be made during the morning announcements for "A junior class meeting tonight at John XX's house (who was White) and then later in the announcements you would hear "A junior class meeting tonight at James XX's house (who was Black). Events such as the prom were organized in this racially-oriented fashion. When I tell this particularly to people from large urban cities they just frown in disbelief. Others think I'm just lying. But those are the things many of my generation from the South had to go through to get to where we are today.

There were other problems that my own kids had to go through to get to where they are today. In Israel my children were accepted as bright kids. Their Israeli teachers didn't come in with the preconceived idea that because of their color, they were stupid. My kids didn't have to deal with that in Israel. When my kids went to school, they were accepted. At times, my daughter Dionn was the only child of color in any class, but she was accepted.

But on our return to the US my children had to face some of the same issues I experienced in the 1970s. The school we chose in Atlanta wanted to put Dionn in remedial classes because they couldn't interpret or understand her academic transcripts. They said, "Oh we don't know how to place her because of her documentation." I knew that she was completing more advanced work in Israel than the kids her age in Atlanta. Despite my frustration, I calmly asked, "Why don't you test her to see where she's supposed to be?" After testing her, they realized she didn't need to be in remedial classes. In fact, she was substantially ahead of her grade level.

These are the negative things many people have to go through to get to achieve their goals and dreams. That's my "Why Cry," we can overcome it all. So these days I try to focus on the good that came from those experiences. Sports have always been something that has always offered a positive influence and added value. It taught me to have good discipline and good character. I wonder in this day of one and done, sitting out college football bowl games or switching professional teams at the drop of the hat, what values professional sports are offering today. And more importantly, what are our kids observing of value from professional athletes? I remember when Charles Barkley had the commercial that said, "I am not a role model." I thought that was interesting because he was a role model whether he liked it or not. It's not something that you ask for as an athlete, but it is something that is bestowed upon you. More importantly, God said "to whom much is given, from him much will be required" (Luke 12:48 NKJV). So, you can't go and say that athletes are not role models for kids. Unfortunately, much of the world has become a world just about "me." It's hard to imagine that the world will continue to become a better place if it remains just about "me."

It's difficult to see that some things have changed very little since I was a teenager and there are still teens out there like me who are going through things to get to a better place. I have gone through a lot in life. So has my sister Mary. Yet, she travels regularly to Africa as a part of an organization that supports schools in Kenya. Even though we grew up in Charlton Grove with nothing, we have traveled around the world a couple of times. I doubt anyone would have thought we would have come from that little house in Charlton Grove to be a brother and sister that have traveled around the world. Clearly that was something we had to go through to get to this stage in life. Oftentimes we just need to take a minute to stop and reflect on what we have gone through to get a true appreciation of where we are now.

THE POWER OF LOVE

"Darkness cannot drive out darkness; only light can do that. Hate cannot drive out hate; only love can do that."

Martin Luther King Jr.

I have been asked many times about the concept of love. Some have asked how one can come from virtually nothing and faced so many trials, but still be focused on love of all people. Even in interviewing friends from this book, several mentioned love. They noted that I have love for people and people have love for me. There is substantial power in love. I have a general goal in life to try to spread love. I'm not sure I really know where that comes from, but in my innermost being, I have a desire to offer love to others.

If I could capture or explain the word love I would use something that came to me one day on a beach in Tel Aviv. Love is made of four powerful letters that capture the complexity and essence of love. First, there is **L** that translates into the concept of "loneliness." Not loneliness in the negative sense; but more of you really need to be isolated within yourself and dig deep into your innermost thoughts to understand exactly who you are. Without truly understanding who you are, I think it's hard to change and become the person you are meant to be or as we say today, your best self. You must move away from others to find yourself; your strengths and your weaknesses.

Second there is **O** or your "openness." You must be able to open yourself up to others and express your inner self to others. You must allow them to really dig down into you to see who you are, so that they can be a friend to you and help you continue to be a better you. Next there is **V** or your "vision." Vision is the epitome of knowing where you are trying to go and what you're trying to do. I'm always trying to be the greatest version of myself that I can be based on what I see in myself. I want to be a child of God that is really doing something positive. I want to be the best father that I can be. I want to be the best friend that I can be. I want to always be going forward in life. Now **E** is where the problem comes in. **E** represents the "expectations" that others have for you or what others always need or see that they want from you. Everybody that you touch in life has an expectation of you, regardless of whether you want to see that or not in them. **E** is someone else's expectation of what they want or what they are going to see if they can get from you or out of you. You must be able to manage your **E's**, because people will always come with an **E** mindset. People have asked me can you love more than one place or person? Can you love Israel the same way you love the US? The answer is yes, you can love more than one place or person but in different ways and for different reasons. I absolutely do. Some have asked, can you love more than one woman? Yes, you can because each person will bring something different into your life. Now you just can't be in love with them at the same time, but you can love more than one person. If you are truly open in life you will always love............you cannot be a person that does not love. My greatest loves have been my wife, children and family.

Now reflecting over the years, one might ask "What has been the expectation of LaVon Mercer?" I would say it's not the expectation of LaVon Mercer, it is the vision of LaVon Mercer. LaVon Mercer's vision is to be the best and go forward in life and help others and be epitome of leaders such Abraham, Jesus, Buddha, Mohammed or whoever you see in a powerful position. I want to be the best at helping people and positively influencing them in any way I can. I want to give off a positive feeling at each interaction and when I leave that person, they will have experienced something positive. For example, you don't have to like me, but I want you to love me in the sense that I'm going to give you love and hopefully you can get something positive from me.

Other's expectations of LaVon have nothing to do with anything because that is their expectation for me. That is what others want me to do, how they want me to be or where they want me to go. That is not really my issue. Sometimes there can be an expectation of you for money, friendship, guidance, a male role model or whatever it is that the person feels they need. Everyone has some sort of expectation of you as a person. Even when family, friends or acquaintances have an expectation of you, your vision is something that they cannot manipulate. Your vision is a distant picture of where you're trying to get to. Your vision must always override the expectations of others.

When I was at UGA there were many, many expectations of me beyond basketball. For some students it was just to be a friend with an athlete so they could connect with and hang out with other athletes. And most of the time I just didn't want that. I had friends like Herman and Bruce Cohen who had gone through some things with me, and they were friends I could really trust. Consequently, there were people at UGA who just couldn't understand why we were so close. Herman and Bruce were not college athletes so it seemed I shouldn't be spending my time with them. But to me that was just stupid because Herman was my big brother and Bruce was in some respects a calming factor. Some people couldn't understand that, but that was their problem.

Each person should be cautious about the influence the expectations that others have on them. People can be very fickle at times and change on you quickly. So, I tend to focus on the vision I have for myself and not the expectations of others. It's the same way with my good friend Reggie Johnson. We've known each other since we were 13 years old. We've gone through some things together. He understands my vision and his expectations of me as a friend will never get in the way of my vision.

Another way to think about this concept of love is, love is constant and not a fleeting emotion. True love allows the expectations of others to align with the vision of the individual. Love will be there at the darkest moments and a person who really loves will not be the person who stands off from you during a trial and laughs at you. Well maybe they won't laugh, but they certainly won't spend time telling others and whispering about your troubles yet offering no support or assistance. I don't ever want to be that person. I guess that's why love is so important to society or maybe even humanity in general. We should always spread love and try our best to access the power of love.

A MAN OF TWO LANDS

"If we are to have peace on earth....... our loyalties must transcend our race, our tribe, our class, and our nation; and this means we must develop a world perspective."

Martin Luther King Jr.

My hope in writing this book was to tell a unique story about a man who really is connected to two different lands; two different cultures. My story is one of rising up out of poverty; essentially rising up from nothing to become something. And in the process of that journey being exposed to a wide range of people, opportunities, cultures and regions of the world. The journey also offered an opportunity to seek and explore my own faith, my own beliefs while seeking to understand and grow in God and as a man. But I guess more important of all, is to find that peace that many seek but are not able to find. On some level, I'm still seeking and searching for the ultimate peace that I now know can only come from a connection with God.

Now don't get me wrong, basketball, the game I love, has been awesome to me. It allowed me to attend college and play professional basketball in foreign lands that for many who come from small rural towns, seem unreal. Traveling to Europe or Asia or Africa seemed far-fetched to me as a kid as I knew just a few kids who had traveled out of the state of GA. It's kind of amazing and funny now to think about how few places I had gone outside of GA. I'm tickled to look back now and think that I ended up being that person that I read about in these old second-hand books who traveled the world on an adventure. Many of us remember seeing Jacques Cousteau exploring underwater reefs around the world or the television show Mutual of Omaha's Wild Kingdom which gave us a glimpse of animal life in the African Serengeti.

I, like many people around me in Metter, had no real concept of the bigger world. Our thoughts were limited to life in our Charlton Grove community and Lillian Street. But with God's blessings, I have had an opportunity to be Metter's Jacque Cousteau of basketball. I have traveled the world playing the game I love. In my travels I was exposed to many different people and offered opportunities that have shaped who I am today. I have had an opportunity to live and grow in what was initially a foreign land to me. I received an opportunity to experience something unique when initially I was simply seeking to continue my basketball career. My basketball career has come full circle to where it all began. My high school jersey was retired in 2018 and the ceremony stirred a range of emotions and memories about where it all began.

Writing this book forced me to dig deep and evaluate my life and to answer two fundamental questions. The first question is "Who is LaVon Mercer?" The second question is "Can a man be from two lands?" The question of who LaVon Mercer seemed simple at the outset, but I found myself spending hours and hours trying to adequately answer that question.

The time devoted to the answer highlights the complexity of the question and some uncertainty as to who I am. I believe I understand who I am, but answering the question forced me to reflect on how others see me and whether I have accomplished the personal goals I set for myself. I'm not thinking about the professional goals because in some respects, I have superseded those professional goals. I like so many, wonder if I have accomplished or made the necessary progress in being the person my family, friends and God need me to be?

Some say that I am a "gentle giant." Several folks interviewed for this book mentioned that term. I take that to mean a person who is humble, respectful and potentially a lion in waiting. A lot of animals like bears have a good and a bad side. Most bears that live in the wild won't bother you until you bother them, or you attack their babies or other family members. The humble bear will not bother you until you bother them.

In our research for this book, we found an article in UGA's Red and Black student newspaper that was published in 1977; over 40 years ago. The article was published during my freshman year at UGA and spoke of me being a shy kid who downplayed my stardom and the accolades that put me in the national spotlight. I was expected to contribute my freshman year since my status was of one of the most highly recruited basketball players from the state of Georgia that year. I decided to do the one thing that was under my control which was to get better. I went back to the basics, the fundamentals of the game and tried to perfect them as a way of improving my game. Life is like that in a lot of ways...keep things basic and work on improving the little things each and every day. The article also said I had "mastered the art of screening questions from sportswriters that could possibly delve beneath the surface and offer a bit of insight" into why we were winless in the SEC. Maybe my easy-going demeanor and unwillingness to always offer a strong (and at times an uninformed) opinion on things when no answer would really be sufficient, resulted in this belief that I'm a giant but gentle. Who knows? But I hope those around me know that being a gentle giant doesn't mean that I will trust everything that you say or do. In life, we must establish a mutual respect and if that is broken, I may continue to talk to you, but you shouldn't confuse that with me trusting you.

Some say I'm a complex person and there are a lot of layers to LaVon Mercer. Many people know me outside of basketball and they have never seen me play. But here is what I do know, I am the same old LaVon that people have known all along. Some people from my hometown have at times labeled me as something special because of my playing in Israel and traveling abroad. Some may even feel that I have gone far above them. I try to tell people that I really haven't. I have traveled a lot more but I'm still the same old person that they probably remember in the early days. I have seen many things that most people will never see in their lifetimes, but I don't use that to elevate myself above others who have not seen those same places. Basically, I want people to smile when they think of me.

Some people in Israel say that I am a legend. I'm in some books that say I'm a legend in sports or a legend in other things. Some have even said I'm revered at the highest levels in Israel. I just don't know about that because the truth of the matter is that titles are placed on you by man and over time, they may be reduced to have little or no meaning. I try not to think too deeply about that kind of title. I try to focus on being humble about everything that I have accomplished. I try to be a person who doesn't ask for anything but focuses on what I can do to help or to add to other people.

Being humble allows you to be open. I would argue that most people who feel they are so much better than others are also the same kind of people who cannot learn anything from others because they can't open themselves up. That's why I must remain open because when I stop taking chances of being open and available to people, I may miss a blessing because it was intended for me to help someone.

I am the same type of person that I have been my entire life and when I'm gone from this earth, I will be disposed of in the same way as others. I will be either buried in the ground or cremated just like everyone else. I truly believe bodies are only vessels that God gave us to use to do something for him. Maybe this book is the beginning of me going out and speaking about him. I just don't know. I have lived on this earth to be a helpmate to anyone who is willing to listen to something positive that I have to say. And I shall always do that and pass love throughout this earth. I believe that is the easiest way to answer the question of "Who is LaVon Mercer?"

The second question, "Can a man really be from two lands?" was much easier to answer. God frequently has an alternative plan for our lives that is different from the one we have. In my case, my personal plan was to become a professional basketball player in the NBA and earn a great living. God's alternative plan for me was to live in Israel and to become more than a professional basketball player. I was blessed to become a naturalized citizen and a beloved member of Israeli society. I was offered the opportunity of immersion into Israeli culture and Israeli history. For that, I am eternally grateful. Yes, I love the US despite its flaws and my many experiences with racism and oppression. Yes, I love it despite my early experiences of extreme poverty and displacement. Because we all know there is no place like home. But I similarly love Israel despite its flaws and worldwide misperceptions. And yes, you can have a second home. So, the answer to the second question, "Can a man be of and love two lands?" The answer is yes. *I am that man.*

WHY CRY?

"Where there is no struggle, there is no strength."

Oprah Winfrey

"If there is no struggle, there is no progress."

Frederick Douglass

"Ease is a greater threat to progress than hardship."

Denzel Washington

I close this book with some thoughts about my personal story and how it relates to some of the events that are going on today around the world. But my thoughts are grounded mostly in observations of America. My life was filled with many challenges and started in a place that many would consider uninhabitable today. That place was one that I will always remember fondly because of the love that was there. There are many kids across America and in countries around the world that come from the same kind of place that I came from, so the real question is WHY CRY? Like me, I hope they will focus on the positives and the lessons learned there. In those early years, I did not know how bad my situation was because many of my friends were living the same way. It was not until later in life that my eyes were opened to differences in living conditions that some experienced and especially those kids who were White. Yet, it seems that it was not the living condition that was important. The more important issue was, what you do when you are faced with those situations and other stumbling blocks or crossroads in life.

I could have very easily decided to quit basketball at an early age because of those initial 10-12-mile walks home from practice. I could have quit when my grandmother really needed me to work after school after my grandfather became ill. I could have also quit when my grandmother died. I could have just moved to New York with my mother and sisters after my grandmother's death and gave up the dream.

I realize now that the attempts to keep me in Metter may not have worked if it had not been for extended family. The plan the Hortons, Collins and Thomas' constructed could have failed and the dream would have been over. Subsequently there would have never been LaVon Mercer scholarship athlete at UGA. Or the plan could have partially worked, and Momma Sarah could have said I think you need to leave now that Herman has graduated. She could have easily decided that my living there was too much for her and that

I needed to find other arrangements. But in each instance either I or those who helped me get to this point, made the decision to not buckle under the pressure and start crying or quit. WHY CRY?

The title of this book "Why Cry" is a metaphor for "Why focus solely on the negative and miss the opportunity?" "Why break down and quit when the alternative to stand up and fight is available to you?" In today's society, there is a focus on equality, yet the outcome of such efforts may be less beneficial than originally intended. Before you begin to think I don't believe in equality, please let me explain. Equality is "the state of being equal in status, rights and opportunities." At the outset, let me be clear, I absolutely believe in equality. But in some regards, the concept of equality has moved to mean that everyone must receive the exact same lot in life. I am not sure if that is how it was intended and that is not my view.

I started out with a terrible lot in life. But eventually I took part in a magical journey of basketball around the world. As I self-reflect, there were many stumbling blocks and forks in the road where I could have just broken down, cried and quit. If I had decided to do so, I would not have allowed God's vision for me to unfold. I could have broken down crying after my grandparent's death. I don't mean crying literally because I did, **but crying in the sense that one quits some aspects of life and refuses to try to overcome the obstacle**. In these instances, crying is not beneficial. Crying is simply an excuse or reason to explain something that you might be unwilling to try to accomplish. In contrast, the fight is beneficial in these situations.

There were so many instances that I could have just cried about the situation and missed the next opportunity. I could have broken down crying and quit basketball during all the losing seasons at UGA. I could have broken down and began crying when I did not make the Spurs roster. I could have broken down crying after the season in Italy when I wasn't able to join the Spurs in the second year. I could have broken down crying and returned to the US when things fell-apart with the Hapoel Tel Aviv team. I could have cried each time we didn't win a EuroLeague Championship.

I ask the question, WHY CRY, because crying or refusing to "suck it up" and try your best to move forward seems to me more commonplace in society today. We have created so many situations to prevent failure and the opportunity to learn the lessons that come with failure. We have created sports leagues for children where everyone receives a participation trophy. I do understand the impact that these trophies have on self-esteem. But receiving a medal or trophy teaches children a more unrealistic lesson that everyone wins at everything in life.

I have won a lot in life. I have also taken far more devastating losses in athletics and life in general. I have experienced extreme poverty and not knowing where my next meal might come from. I have had to go fishing just to eat that day. I have had to pull plants out of the ground just to be able to eat that day. I have had to stay in a college dorm during the breaks by myself because I didn't have a ride or money to go home. In all those situations, *I decided not to cry but to stand up and move forward.*

I realize there are situations that sometimes one just cannot overcome without help. I acknowledge those situations and the devastation they can cause. I am simply asking that we stop making excuses and placing blame on others for our losses. Losses are part of life and they cannot always be explained by this group or that group holding one down. At each turn we have an opportunity to cry and self-destruct or dig deep and fight. Regardless of the many challenges that I have faced in life or the negativity that I have experienced, I have always decided to fight rather than cry.

If you are someone with a similar background or who is currently experiencing major life challenges, I encourage you to reach out to others for assistance. I also encourage you to avoid making excuses and placing blame on others. I encourage you to refuse to cry and simply stand up and fight to overcome. You will learn more from the fight and be better for the experience. The fight is in you and you must find a way to tap into the fight and move forward with life's challenges. So, why cry when your energy would be better utilized in the fight; WHY CRY?

Photo Credits

All photos taken while at The University of Georgia were used with permission from The Red and Black Newspaper Archives which are part of the Georgia Historic Newspaper Archives. Photos in the Georgia Historic Newspaper Archives are either in the public domain or permission has been granted by the copyright owner for digital distribution for personal or educational use.

All photos taken while playing for the Maccabi Tel Aviv Basketball Club were part of a program created for Mr. Mercer's retirement ceremony. All photos were used with permission from Maccabi Tel Aviv Basketball Club.

All photos taken at Camp Coleman were used with permission from Mr. Bobby Harris.

All photos of the Thomas family are from the Michaela Thomas Ellis collection and were used with permission.

All other photos are from the LaVon Mercer collection and were used with permission.

ABOUT THE AUTHORS

LaVon Curtis Mercer was born in Metter, GA where he graduated from Metter High School in 1976. Following his senior at Metter High School he was named the Georgia High School Association Player and a high school All American. He received over 300 scholarship offers and eventually accepted a full athletic scholarship to play basketball at The University of Georgia. He still holds the UGA record for field goal percentage in a season (.643) and for a career (.602). He is also holds the record for most career blocks (327) at UGA. After a stellar career at UGA, he was selected in the third round (60th overall) of the 1980 NBA draft by the San Antonio Spurs. At the urging of the Spurs, he played one year in the Italian basketball league and planned to return to US to begin his NBA career. But as fate would have it, he received an opportunity to play basketball in Israel. In Israel he played for Hapoel Tel Aviv (1981–1988) and Maccabi Tel Aviv (1988–1995). During that time his teams won six Israeli Champions (1989, 1990, 1991, 1992, 1994, 1995) and five Israeli State Cups (1984, 1989, 1990, 1991, 1994). In 1989 his Maccabi team reached the EuroLeague finals and in 1991 they reached the EuroLeague semifinals. Mr. Mercer is a naturalized citizen of Israel and served in the Israeli Defense Force from 1987-1994. LaVon and his wife Madeline have three wonderful adult children; Dionn, Alex and Gabby. He currently lives with his wife Madeline in Douglasville, GA.

Charles Ellis, Jr., PhD was born in Claxton, GA. As a preteen he moved to Metter, GA where he graduated from Metter High School in 1985. After graduation he attended The University of Georgia in Athens, GA where he received a BSED and MA in Communication Sciences & Disorders in 1990 and 1992 respectively. In 2005 he received a PhD in Rehabilitation Science from the University of Florida in Gainesville, FL. He currently lives in Raleigh, NC with his wife Michaela and daughter Hailee.

Connect with LaVon on Facebook @:

Why Cry LaVon Mercer

If you are interested in hearing more about the life of LaVon and his experiences in Israel, please feel free to contact him at: **whycrydawg33@gmail.com**